TABLE OF CONTENT

Word from the Author

Do you know that feeling? The one where it seems no matter what you do, you just can't break free. You're working hard, trying everything, but it feels like you're running in quicksand. The harder you push, the deeper you sink.

It's frustrating, right? It's more than just feeling lazy or unmotivated—it's that crushing sense that progress isn't even possible, like something invisible is holding you back.

I've been there. And here's what I want you to know: It's not your fault.

You see, our brains are wired to keep us stuck in the familiar, even when we want to move forward. But you don't need to stay stuck. And the way out isn't some massive life overhaul—it's in the small, intentional steps that create real momentum.

This book isn't about grand gestures or impossible-to-keep promises. **"Unstuck: Small Changes, Big Results"** is a roadmap for taking those tiny steps that lead to major breakthroughs. We'll uncover the habits and thought patterns that have you stuck and replace them with practical, bite-sized actions that help you build progress. One step at a time.

The best part? You don't need to get it perfect. You just need to start.

The fact that you picked up this book tells me you're ready. Ready to make the changes you've been waiting for. So, let's begin this journey together. We'll take it step by step, and before you know it, those small wins will add up to big results.

Antonio Garrido Caballero

Chapter 1: What Does Stuck Feel Like?

The Fog of Inertia: Where Progress Disappears

It creeps in quietly—at first, you barely notice. You go through your usual routine: wake up, grab your phone, and scroll through your notifications. The day stretches ahead of you, full of things you know you should do, things you meant to do yesterday, things that will pile up if you don't get to them soon.

But instead of diving in, you linger. Just five more minutes. **Maybe you'll feel more motivated if you wait.** But the minutes pass, and instead of energy, you feel a strange heaviness—a fog settling over you, clouding every intention.

This is what being stuck feels like: **an invisible force keeping you rooted in place**, even when you want nothing more than to move forward. It's not just about laziness or procrastination—it's something deeper.

It's paralysis.

The Psychology of Stuck: Why Your Brain Prefers the Familiar

Here's what most people don't realize: **Your brain isn't built for change—it's built for survival.** Thousands of years ago, survival meant staying with the familiar—because unfamiliar things (a strange path, an unfamiliar tribe) often signaled danger. Your brain evolved to treat uncertainty as a threat, triggering anxiety and hesitation to keep you safe.

Today, those same mental mechanisms are still at work—but the threats are different. **Now, uncertainty looks like an unwritten email, an unfinished task, or a decision you don't know how to make.** Your brain doesn't distinguish between "real danger" and "uncomfortable new experiences." It just sends the same signal: *Stay put. Do nothing. Avoid discomfort.*

This is why stuckness feels so paralyzing. **It's not just mental—it's biological.** Your brain, in its attempt to protect you, traps you in a loop of avoidance, comfort, and inaction.

The Emotional Toll of Being Stuck

The hardest part of being stuck isn't just the inaction—it's the way it makes you **doubt yourself.** After a few days (or weeks, or months) of struggling to move forward, you start to believe the problem isn't situational—it's *you*.

Why can't I just get moving?
What's wrong with me?

And that voice, that internal critic, gets louder every day. It whispers that you're lazy, unmotivated, or incapable—that you'll never catch up, never get it right, never become the person you want to be.

This creates what psychologists call a **shame loop**. The more you try and fail, the more shame you feel. And the more shame you feel, the harder it becomes to even attempt something new. You convince yourself that trying isn't worth the risk of more failure. So you stay stuck. **And the longer you stay stuck, the heavier it feels.**

Micro-Decisions and the Fear of the Wrong Move

Being stuck often isn't about one big thing—it's about a thousand **tiny decisions** you don't know how to make. Should you answer that email or tackle your to-do list? Should you clean the house or start that side project you've been putting off? What if you do one thing and regret it later?

These small choices start to feel overwhelming, and your brain—trying to keep you safe—whispers: *Do nothing for now. Wait until you feel more certain.*

But certainty never comes. And so you sit there, waiting for motivation that refuses to arrive, **stuck in the limbo between indecision and inaction.**

This is how your brain keeps you trapped: **by making every step feel riskier than it really is.** But here's the thing: **The only way out is through.**

You don't need certainty to move forward. You just need to start.

How to Recognize the Signs of Stuckness

Stuckness doesn't always look the way you think it will. Here are a few signs you might be more stuck than you realize:

- **Procrastination disguised as productivity.** (Cleaning your workspace instead of starting the project.)
- **Emotional numbness.** (You're going through the motions, but nothing feels meaningful.)
- **Overplanning.** (You're stuck in the preparation phase, waiting for the "perfect" time to begin.)
- **Decision fatigue.** (You're exhausted before you even start, overwhelmed by the choices ahead.)
- **Avoidance.** (You distract yourself with Netflix, social media, or busywork to avoid what really matters.)

Does any of this sound familiar? If so, you're not alone. **This is what stuck looks like. And it's not your fault.**

How to Break Free: Small Wins, Big Shifts

Getting unstuck doesn't require a grand plan. In fact, **the key to breaking free is to start small—so small it feels almost pointless.**

The reason is simple: **Small actions bypass your brain's fear response.** They're safe. They're manageable. And once you take one small step, the next one becomes easier. This is called **the "micro-movement effect"—tiny wins that create momentum.**

Think of it this way: **You don't climb a mountain in one leap. You take it one step at a time.** And every small step, no matter how insignificant it seems, brings you closer to the top.

Action Step: Your First Micro-Movement

Let's try something simple. **Pick one tiny action** you can take right now—something that takes no more than five minutes.

- **Send a text** to someone you've been meaning to contact.
- **Write down** the first task for tomorrow.
- **Walk outside** for two minutes to clear your mind.

The goal isn't to solve everything. **The goal is to move, even a little.** Because every small movement chips away at the inertia keeping you stuck. And with every step you take, your brain learns: *It's safe to move forward.*

Why Small Steps Matter: The Neuroscience of Progress

Here's what makes small wins so powerful: **They create dopamine, the brain's reward chemical.** Dopamine reinforces behaviors, which means that every small success makes it more likely you'll take another step. Over time, **these tiny victories build momentum**, and momentum builds progress.

It's like a snowball rolling down a hill—each movement adds weight and speed, until suddenly, you're unstoppable.

This is the science of stuck: **The more you move, the easier movement becomes.**

Closing Thought: Begin Where You Are

You don't need to have it all figured out. You don't need a perfect plan or the right mindset. **All you need is to begin—right where you are, with what you have.**

Stuckness isn't a sign that you've failed. It's just a signal that something needs to shift. And the good news? **You have everything you need to make that shift, one small step at a time.**

The only way out is through. And the first step? **It starts now.**

Neuroscience Insight:

The sensation of being stuck comes from the prefrontal cortex, the part of the brain responsible for decision-making and goal-setting. When overwhelmed or anxious, the amygdala (the brain's fear center) hijacks this process, making it harder to act. This is called amygdala hijacking, leading to mental paralysis.

- ***Practical Takeaway:*** Small actions activate the dopaminergic pathways, slowly rewiring the brain and reducing the fear response over time.

Case Study: Lisa's Loop of Indecision

Lisa's alarm buzzed sharply at 6:30 a.m., just like it did every weekday morning. She groaned, slapped the snooze button, and buried herself deeper into the covers. **Five more minutes wouldn't change anything.** It was another day, the same as yesterday, and the same as the hundreds of days before that.

For six years, Lisa's life had **followed a monotonous rhythm.** She worked in the operations department of a mid-sized company, where she filed reports, answered emails, and attended meetings where her ideas were politely dismissed. Her workdays were a blur—one email led to another meeting, which led to more reports. And at the end of each day, she would walk home feeling drained but strangely restless, wondering, *Is this all there is?*

Lisa knew deep down that she **wanted more.** She had always dreamed of opening an online art shop—selling custom prints, handcrafted designs, and paintings she made during the weekends. **Art had been her passion since childhood,** but life had pulled her in a safer direction. She majored in business at her parents' urging—*something practical,* they had said. After graduation, one job offer led to another, and suddenly **years had slipped away.**

The What-If Spiral

Almost every night, Lisa would lie awake imagining what it would be like to quit her job and start her art business. *I'll quit next month,* she'd tell herself. *I just need a little more time to plan.* She spent hours **researching websites, marketing strategies, and other artists who had found success.** She bookmarked pages, created spreadsheets, and filled a notebook with ideas.

But every morning brought **a new set of excuses**: *What if the shop fails? What if I waste all my savings? What if no one buys my work?* And, worst of all: *What if I'm not talented enough?*

The more she thought about the risks, the more **paralyzed she became.** Every day felt like another missed opportunity, but **staying in her safe, familiar routine** felt easier than confronting the terrifying unknown.

Months rolled by. Then years. And still, Lisa sat at the same desk, typing reports and updating spreadsheets that no one seemed to care about. **The dreams she once cherished began to feel distant, even impossible.**

The Weight of Inaction

Lisa noticed the subtle signs of burnout creeping in. **Her motivation dwindled.** Even tasks that used to be easy felt overwhelming. She'd sit at her desk and stare at her computer, her hands hovering over the keyboard as her mind wandered. Some mornings, she struggled to get out of bed, **dreading the thought of spending another day doing something that didn't matter to her.**

A voice in the back of her mind grew louder: *You're wasting time. You're running out of chances.* It whispered constantly, following her on her morning commute and creeping in during meetings. **Lisa felt trapped in a loop, but the fear of failure kept her stuck.** As much as she hated her current situation, the idea of stepping into the unknown felt even scarier.

And so, every day, she told herself the same thing: *Tomorrow. I'll quit tomorrow.*

The Turning Point: A Simple Question

One Saturday afternoon, Lisa met her old friend Ava for coffee. They hadn't seen each other in months, and Lisa spent most of the conversation **venting about work—**

how bored she was, how she felt like she was slowly wasting away in her job, and how she wished she could finally start her art shop.

Ava listened patiently and then asked a simple question: **"How long are you going to wait?"**

Lisa froze, her coffee cup suspended in mid-air. The words hit her like a punch to the gut. She had no answer. How long *was* she going to wait? Another month? Another year? **Another six years?**

That night, **Ava's question echoed in Lisa's mind.** She realized that waiting wasn't keeping her safe—it was draining her life, one day at a time. The fear of failure had become **a cage, trapping her in a version of life she no longer wanted.**

The truth was, she wasn't stuck because of her job, her savings, or the economy—**she was stuck because she was too afraid to move.**

Taking the First Step

The next morning, Lisa sat at her kitchen table with her notebook and a cup of coffee. She stared at the page for a long time, **her heart racing.** The voice of her inner critic whispered: *You'll never succeed. Who do you think you are?*

But **this time, she didn't listen.** Instead, she wrote down **one small step** she could take: Create a simple Etsy store by the end of the week. Not a perfect, fully designed shop—just a basic store with a few items. **She didn't need to get it perfect; she just needed to start.**

And she did. By the following weekend, Lisa had uploaded her first three art prints. **The shop wasn't flawless, but it was real.** For the first time in years, she felt a flicker of excitement—and relief. It wasn't the grand launch she had envisioned, but it was a start.

Progress Through Imperfection

Over the next few weeks, Lisa committed to **small daily actions**—responding to customer messages, tweaking her product descriptions, experimenting with social media posts. **Each small win gave her the confidence to take the next step.**

She still had doubts, of course. There were moments when she wondered if she'd made a mistake. But with every sale—whether big or small—she proved to herself that **the fear had been lying all along.** The path wasn't easy, but it was hers.

Lisa realized that **momentum didn't come from waiting for the perfect moment.** It came from taking small, imperfect steps forward. And with each step, the grip of fear loosened just a little more.

Lisa's story isn't about a sudden breakthrough or a grand success—it's about **the quiet courage to move, even when fear tries to hold you back.** The truth is, waiting for the perfect moment will only keep you stuck. **There's never a perfect moment to start.** But every time you take action—no matter how small—you reclaim your power.

Lisa learned that **fear will always be part of the journey,** but it doesn't have to control her. Progress comes not from being fearless, but from **taking the next step anyway.**

And so, step by step, **Lisa built the life she wanted.** Not perfectly, but intentionally—and that was enough.

Chapter 2: The Comparison Trap

The Silent Game Everyone's Playing

You don't plan to compare yourself to others. It just... happens. You open your social media feed and suddenly, **everyone else's life looks brighter, bigger, and more successful** than yours. Promotions, vacations, happy relationships—while you sit there, scrolling, wondering what they know that you don't.

Comparison is sneaky. It whispers: *You're not doing enough. You're falling behind. Everyone else has figured out something you haven't.* And before you know it, you're **measuring your self-worth** against someone else's highlight reel.

The Neuroscience Behind Comparison: Why It Feels So Awful

Here's what makes comparison so hard to shake: **It's wired into your brain.**

From an evolutionary perspective, comparing ourselves to others was a survival mechanism. In the past, **belonging to a tribe meant life or death.** Our ancestors needed to know how they ranked in the group—**who had more power, who had more resources, who was thriving.** Keeping an eye on others was a way to learn what worked and adapt to avoid falling behind.

But the world today is different. We're no longer in survival mode, but **our brains haven't caught up.** We still instinctively compare ourselves to others, except now, the comparisons are endless—**a never-ending stream of filtered perfection and success.**

When you compare, your brain activates the **same dopamine pathways** involved in addiction. At first, the comparison offers a quick reward—"Oh, they got a promotion? That means it's possible for me too." But the more you scroll, the **further your self-worth drops**. Your brain becomes trapped in a cycle:

1. **Trigger:** You see someone's success.

2. **Comparison:** You feel inadequate.

3. **Outcome:** You promise yourself you'll do more— try harder, achieve faster—just to keep up.

4. **Repeat.**

This loop leaves you feeling drained, discontent, and stuck in **a constant state of "not enough."**

The Highlight Reel Illusion

The worst part of comparison? **You're comparing your messy, behind-the-scenes life to someone else's carefully curated highlight reel.**

What you don't see behind that polished vacation photo is the argument that happened on the flight. What you don't hear about the new job is the anxiety that keeps them awake at night. And what no one tells you about success is that it doesn't solve every problem—it just brings new ones.

Everyone struggles. But comparison hides that truth, making it feel like you're the only one falling short.

The Cost of Constant Comparison

The more you compare, the harder it becomes to see **your own progress.** You stop noticing your small wins because they don't look as impressive as someone else's achievements. You dismiss the things that bring you joy because they're not *big enough* to share.

And over time, comparison **shrinks your life**—turning joy into jealousy, gratitude into envy, and progress into pressure. You start chasing things not because they matter to you, but because you think they'll make you feel "enough."

Breaking Free from the Comparison Trap

The good news? **You don't have to stay trapped.** Comparison may be wired into your brain, but **you can rewire the way you respond.**

Here are a few ways to start:

1. Curate Your Input: Choose What You Feed Your Brain

Your brain absorbs whatever you expose it to. If scrolling through social media leaves you feeling worse, **set**

boundaries. Unfollow people who make you feel less-than, and follow those who inspire or uplift you.

Remember: **You have control over what you consume.** Curating your input isn't about avoiding reality—it's about **protecting your peace.**

---

2. Celebrate Your Own Wins—Even the Tiny Ones

One reason comparison feels so heavy is because **we're not trained to celebrate small victories.** But progress is progress, no matter how small.

Keep a **"win journal"** where you jot down even the tiniest steps forward:

- Sent that overdue email?
- Took a walk instead of doom-scrolling?
- Made it through the day? **That counts.**

When you celebrate your wins, you **train your brain to notice progress.** And the more you notice your own progress, the less you need to measure it against someone else's.

---

3. Practice Gratitude for Where You Are

Gratitude rewires your brain to focus on **what's good in your life right now,** instead of what's missing. Start by listing three things you're grateful for each day—small things that bring you joy, like a hot cup of coffee or a good conversation.

Gratitude doesn't mean ignoring your struggles. It just means recognizing that, even on the hardest days, there's something worth appreciating.

---

4. Define Success on Your Own Terms

One of the reasons comparison feels so heavy is because **we let other people define what success looks like.** But success isn't one-size-fits-all.

What does success mean to *you*? Maybe it's creating time for your passions. Maybe it's nurturing meaningful relationships. Or maybe success is just getting through today with kindness and grace. **The only definition of success that matters is your own.**

Reflection: What Are You Chasing?

Take a moment to ask yourself: **Am I chasing things that matter to me, or things I think I should want?**

If the life you're building is based on other people's expectations, you'll always feel stuck—because **their version of success will never fit you perfectly.**

But when you let go of comparison and start living for yourself, **you make space for joy, progress, and fulfillment.** You stop waiting for permission to feel happy—and start giving that permission to yourself.

Closing Thought: You Are Already Enough

You don't need to wait until you catch up to someone else's timeline to feel good about your life. You are **enough right now, exactly as you are.**

The next time you catch yourself comparing, take a deep breath and remind yourself: **Your progress is real. Your journey is valid.**

Life isn't a race, and you don't need to keep up with anyone but yourself.

So, **what small step can you take today, just for you?**

Neuroscience Insight:
The ventral striatum, the brain's reward center, is highly active when we compare ourselves to others—especially on social media. It releases dopamine, making us crave the validation that comparisons seem to offer, but it also makes negative comparisons painful.

- *Practical Takeaway*: Limiting exposure to comparison triggers and replacing external validation with internal wins helps reduce the craving for social comparison

Jakes Case Study

Jake hadn't planned to spend hours scrolling through Instagram every night—it just kind of happened. It had started innocently enough: **checking in on friends** from high school, following travel influencers, and keeping up with memes. But **as the months rolled by, it turned into a nightly ritual**—one that left him feeling worse about himself each time.

At first, Jake convinced himself it was just entertainment. But with every **perfectly curated vacation photo, glowing career announcement, or engagement post**, the **tightness in his chest grew heavier.** Friends he hadn't spoken to in years seemed to be **leaping from one achievement to the next**, while he remained in the same place—working a job that paid the bills but never lit him up, and living in a small apartment with a view of the parking lot.

One night, Jake's thumb froze mid-scroll. There it was— a post from an old classmate: **"Just bought my first house!"** The caption was cheerful, filled with hashtags about #adulting and #blessed. Jake stared at the picture of his friend standing on the porch of a beautiful, suburban home, grinning from ear to ear, keys in hand. **A pang of envy** settled in his chest, sharp and familiar.

"Why can't that be me?" Jake thought, his heart sinking. He closed the app, tossing his phone onto the pillow beside him. Lying on his back, he stared at the ceiling, his mind spiraling. *I'm 30 and still renting. I haven't even*

started saving for a house. Everyone else is moving forward, and I'm stuck in the same place.

The more Jake scrolled, the deeper his **sense of failure grew.** It didn't matter that his job provided financial stability or that he had supportive friends. **In the shadow of everyone else's achievements, nothing in his own life seemed good enough.**

Days turned into weeks, and **the habit of comparison took hold.** Every night, Jake found himself **falling further down the rabbit hole**—scrolling endlessly through social media feeds filled with people who seemed to have it all figured out. Each time he opened the app, **the familiar knot tightened in his chest.**

The Breaking Point

Jake hit **his breaking point** one night when he saw an announcement from another friend: *"We're expecting!"* The photo showed a glowing couple holding a pair of baby shoes, surrounded by well-wishes in the comments. Jake felt a wave of **inadequacy crash over him.**

They're having babies. Buying houses. Getting promotions. Meanwhile, what have I done? The voice in his head was relentless. **Every achievement he saw online felt like a reminder of what he hadn't accomplished.** He began dreading social gatherings, convinced that everyone was further ahead in life than he was.

One night, after hours of scrolling, **Jake broke down.** He felt heavy with the thought that **he was failing at life.**

A New Perspective

The following weekend, Jake visited his cousin Claire, a psychotherapist, who quickly picked up on his frustration. After he vented about feeling left behind, Claire offered a piece of advice that **shifted everything**:

"Social media isn't real life, Jake. It's a highlight reel. You're comparing your everyday moments to everyone else's best moments. That's not a fair comparison."

The words **hit Jake harder than he expected.** He had always known, on some level, that social media was curated—but hearing it said aloud made it **feel real**. Claire continued:

"You don't see the whole picture. You see their promotions, not their bad days. You see their engagements, not their doubts. Everyone struggles, Jake, even if they don't post about it."

A Small Shift

Jake went home that night and **deleted Instagram from his phone.** For the first time in months, he sat quietly in his apartment without the constant need to check his feed. The silence was uncomfortable at first—he wasn't used to being alone with his thoughts. But over time, the **absence of comparison gave him room to breathe.**

In the weeks that followed, Jake began **focusing on his own small wins.** He made a list of things he was proud of—things that didn't seem like much but **were meaningful to him.** He went for morning jogs, called up old friends, and set **simple, achievable goals.**

One day, he completed his first 5K run. The finish line wasn't grand, and there were no cameras or hashtags— just **a quiet sense of satisfaction.** And in that moment, Jake realized something:

The race he thought he was losing **was one he didn't need to run.** Everyone's timeline was different, and **progress didn't have to be public to matter.**

The Lesson

Jake's story isn't about giving up on goals—it's about **learning to measure progress on your own terms.** When he stopped **comparing his journey to someone else's highlight reel,** he found freedom in the small victories that had been there all along.

He learned that **life isn't a competition**, and there's no "right" way to succeed. The only timeline that mattered was his own. And with each jog, phone call, and personal achievement, Jake realized that **he was exactly where he needed to be.**

Take the Leap

You've spent long enough measuring yourself against someone else's story. But here's the truth: you're not behind, you're not falling short—you're exactly where you need to be.

The only life worth comparing yourself to is your own, and today is the day to make that life count. It's time to stop scrolling and start living. Each small action you take from here is a declaration that you're enough, just as you are.

Chapter 3: The Myth of Big Lives

The Illusion of "Making It Big"

We've all been told the same story. The story of **success measured in size**—the bigger the achievement, the more valuable the person. It's the idea that if you're not chasing a promotion, launching a business, buying a bigger house, or earning awards, you're somehow falling short.

In this story, **"small" lives—those lived quietly, away from the spotlight—are treated like failures**. If your dreams don't shake the world, if your name isn't celebrated, if your life is ordinary, does it still matter?

This is the **myth of big lives**—the lie that tells us **only the extraordinary has meaning.**

How the Myth Keeps You Stuck

The myth of big lives creates an **all-or-nothing mindset**: If you're not doing something extraordinary, why bother at all? This way of thinking is dangerous because it paralyzes us. **Why take small steps if they'll never lead to greatness? Why start at all if the goal feels too far away?**

So you sit there, waiting. Waiting for the right moment, the perfect idea, or the kind of inspiration that only seems to visit other people. And while you wait for your "big" moment, **life slips quietly by.**

The Hidden Costs of Big Lives

What no one tells you about big lives is that they come with **unseen trade-offs.**

- **Success brings pressure:** The higher you climb, the harder you have to work to stay at the top.

- **Achievement demands sacrifice:** Behind every extraordinary success is a **hidden cost—time, relationships, peace of mind.**

- **Comparison sneaks in:** The more you achieve, the more you notice others who seem to have done more, making it difficult to feel satisfied.

Many people who achieve "big" lives confess that **it didn't bring the happiness they expected.** Success can feel hollow if it's not aligned with who you are.

And here's the truth: **Bigger isn't always better.** Sometimes, it's just bigger.

The Beauty of Small Lives

There's a different kind of success—**one that's quieter, but just as valuable.** It's the kind of success that shows up in **small moments, meaningful conversations, and personal victories.**

- It's the joy of spending time with people you love.

- It's the satisfaction of creating something—just for you.

- It's the peace that comes from knowing that you're living in alignment with your values, even if no one else notices.

Small lives don't make headlines, but **they create meaning** in ways that big lives often can't. **There's beauty in the ordinary**—in being present, in showing kindness, in finding joy in small things.

Why We Dismiss Small Successes

So why do we ignore the beauty of small lives? Why do we dismiss our progress unless it's monumental? It comes down to **visibility.** Society has taught us that if something isn't seen and celebrated, it doesn't matter. But the truth is, **the most important things often happen quietly.**

Think about it:

- A kind word can change someone's day.

- A small gesture of care can create ripples you'll never see.

- Showing up for yourself—even when no one notices—is an act of quiet bravery.

The world doesn't need to know about every success for it to matter. **The impact of your life isn't measured by its visibility.**

Redefining Success on Your Terms

What if success wasn't about **being bigger or better**? What if success was simply about **living fully and authentically**—on your own terms?

Take a moment to reflect:

- What does success mean to **you**?

- What brings you joy, even if no one else notices?

- What kind of life feels meaningful—not for the world, but for yourself?

When you let go of the myth of big lives, **you free yourself to live deeply in the present.** You no longer need to chase external approval to feel whole. **Your life doesn't need to be extraordinary to be meaningful.**

Action Step: Define Your Version of Success

Here's a simple exercise: **Write down three things** that make you feel fulfilled. They don't need to be big—they just need to feel meaningful to you.

- Maybe it's making time to read a book you love.

- Maybe it's nurturing a relationship that matters.

- Maybe it's finding a small moment of peace in your day.

These things are **your version of success.** Hold onto them. The next time you feel pressure to chase something bigger, **remind yourself of what truly matters.**

Living Fully in a Small Life

The myth of big lives teaches us that **more is always better**—more success, more achievement, more recognition. But the truth is, **you don't need more to be enough.**

Your life, exactly as it is, holds meaning. The small moments are not distractions from real life—they **are** real life. **Success isn't out there—it's already here, waiting to be noticed.**

When you let go of the need for bigger and better, **you make room for joy, connection, and peace.** And in the end, isn't that what success is really about?

Closing Thought: Your Life Is Enough

There's nothing wrong with dreaming big—but **your worth isn't tied to the size of your dreams.** You are enough, exactly as you are.

The next time you catch yourself chasing someone else's version of success, pause. **Take a breath, and remind yourself:**

You are already living a life that matters.

Neuroscience Insight:
The **default mode network (DMN)** in the brain activates when we ruminate about our life and compare it to idealized versions. This network makes us **imagine "what if" scenarios**, creating pressure to live an extraordinary life.

- **Practical Takeaway:** Mindfulness practices deactivate the DMN, helping us stay grounded in **the present moment** rather than chasing grand achievements.

Case Study: Sophia's Search for Meaning

Sophia's life looked **perfect on paper**. At thirty-two, she had earned two degrees from prestigious universities, climbed the corporate ladder, and landed a managerial position at a well-known marketing firm. **Her apartment had floor-to-ceiling windows with a view of the skyline,** and her Instagram feed was filled with photos from work trips to Paris, weekend getaways, and networking events.

From the outside, Sophia seemed to be living the dream. But **inside, she felt hollow**.

The Unspoken Emptiness

Every morning, Sophia went through the same routine—an oat milk latte, 15 minutes of guided meditation, and a quick scroll through emails before heading to the office. But **something had shifted**. The spark that used to come with landing new clients and hitting quarterly goals had dimmed.

One evening, after wrapping up another project, she sat on her couch, staring at the city lights. *Why doesn't this feel as good as it should?* she wondered. Sophia had **achieved everything she had set out to do**, yet **the emptiness lingered**.

She thought about her friends who seemed genuinely happy. **Her college roommate, Mia,** had left a law career to become a yoga instructor. Another friend had downsized to a tiny house and opened a small pottery shop. **They weren't chasing accolades or promotions—yet they seemed fulfilled.** Meanwhile, **Sophia couldn't shake the feeling that something was missing.**

When Success Isn't Enough

Sophia tried filling the void with more work. She **signed up for leadership workshops**, volunteered to take on additional projects, and even started networking for a potential promotion. But the more she chased external success, **the more restless she became**.

She thought: *Maybe I just need to achieve one more thing. Then I'll feel content.* But even as she collected more titles and awards, **the emptiness persisted.** It was as if she had built **a beautiful, towering structure with no foundation** underneath it.

One night, after yet another work event, Sophia broke down. **Sitting in her car in the parking lot, tears streamed down her face.** She felt guilty for feeling this way—after all, she had everything she thought she'd ever wanted. **Why wasn't it enough?**

A Simple Conversation

The next weekend, Sophia visited her grandmother—a kind, soft-spoken woman who had lived in the same small house for 50 years. Sitting on the porch with cups of tea, **Sophia opened up about her restlessness**.

"I don't understand it, Grandma," she said. "I've worked so hard, achieved everything on my list. But I still feel... lost."

Her grandmother smiled gently, placing a hand on hers. **"Happiness isn't something you chase, Sophia,"** she said. **"It's something you find in the small things."**

Those words hit Sophia in a way she hadn't expected. For years, she had believed that fulfillment was waiting at the next milestone—the next job title, the next salary bump, the next big thing. But **what if happiness wasn't in the big moments after all?**

Finding Joy in the Small Things

Over the next few months, **Sophia began to shift her focus.** Instead of filling her schedule with more tasks and projects, she started looking for **small moments of joy.**

She made a habit of taking morning walks in the park, **leaving her phone behind** to simply enjoy the sounds of birds and the crisp morning air. On Sunday afternoons, she baked cookies with her niece, reveling in the sticky mess of flour and chocolate. And every night before bed, she wrote down **three things she was grateful for**—no matter how small.

The joy wasn't immediate or overwhelming. It didn't come with fireworks or applause. But over time, **the restlessness faded**, replaced by a quiet contentment she hadn't known she was missing.

The Realization

Sophia realized that **she had spent years chasing a life that looked impressive** but didn't feel meaningful. Her success had been based on **external validation**—what others thought of her, what society deemed important. But **meaning wasn't something she could find outside**

herself. It was something she had to build, moment by moment, from the inside out.

And those small, quiet moments? **They were the foundation she'd been missing all along.**

The Lesson

Sophia's story isn't about giving up on ambition—it's about **redefining what success means.** There's nothing wrong with chasing dreams or striving for achievements. But **fulfillment doesn't come from checking off a list of accomplishments.** It comes from **building a life that feels right, even if it doesn't look extraordinary.**

Sophia learned that **the myth of big lives is just that—a myth.** Life isn't meant to be lived in grand, cinematic moments. It's meant to be experienced in **the small, imperfect moments**—the walks in the park, the laughter over dinner, the quiet moments of reflection.

She discovered that **she didn't need to chase meaning—it had been there all along, waiting to be noticed.**

Chapter 4: The Weight of Invisible Efforts

When Hard Work Feels Like It's Disappearing

Have you ever poured your heart into something—an assignment, a relationship, or a project—only for it to go unnoticed? You stay up late, push yourself, make sacrifices. And when you finally finish, the world just moves on as if nothing happened. **No applause. No recognition. Just silence.**

It stings, doesn't it? The weight of working so hard without anyone noticing. It makes you wonder: *Does any of this even matter?*

The truth is, **invisible efforts**—the work no one sees, the care that goes unacknowledged—can feel crushing. Over time, it leaves you exhausted, questioning whether it's worth trying at all. But what if there's more to invisible efforts than meets the eye?

The Psychology of Feeling Unseen

There's a reason we crave recognition: **Validation is wired into the human brain.** From a young age, we learn that being acknowledged—whether by teachers, parents, or peers—means we're doing something right. It becomes a feedback loop: **Do good, get noticed, feel good.**

But invisible efforts disrupt that loop. You work hard, but there's no feedback, no celebration. Without that external validation, your brain starts to wonder: *Why bother?*

This is known as **reward deprivation**—when the lack of recognition makes even meaningful work feel pointless. And when that feeling drags on, it often leads to burnout. It's exhausting to keep showing up when **no one seems to notice.**

Why Invisible Efforts Matter More Than You Think

Here's the thing no one tells you: **Invisible efforts aren't wasted—they're foundational.** Just because no one notices your work doesn't mean it's meaningless. Some of the most important things in life happen quietly, without an audience.

- **A teacher stays late grading papers.** The students may never thank them, but the work shapes futures.

- **A parent listens patiently to their child's worries.** The child might not remember the conversation, but it builds trust.

- **A kind word offered at the right moment** may seem insignificant, but it could change someone's day—or even their life.

Invisible efforts create **ripples—impact you can't always see in the moment.**

The Danger of Chasing Only Visible Wins

When you only chase achievements that others can see, **you rob yourself of deeper meaning.** If everything you do is motivated by how it will look to others, you become a performer in your own life—always on stage, always waiting for applause.

But life isn't a performance. And the moments that matter most often **don't come with an audience.**

If you define success only by recognition, you'll end up **exhausted, empty, and stuck**—constantly chasing validation that never feels like enough.

How to Find Meaning in Invisible Efforts

So how do you stay motivated when no one notices your hard work? How do you find joy in your efforts, even when they seem to disappear into the background? Here are a few ways:

1. Shift Your Focus from Outcome to Process

Instead of focusing on whether someone notices your work, **focus on the act of doing it.**

- If you're writing, enjoy the process of putting words on the page.

- If you're helping someone, appreciate the fact that you showed up.

When you shift your focus from outcomes to the process, **the work itself becomes the reward.**

---

2. Create a Ritual to Acknowledge Yourself

If no one else acknowledges your hard work, **you can do it for yourself.**

- At the end of each day, write down three things you accomplished—no matter how small.

- Celebrate small wins, even if it's just with a cup of tea or a quiet moment of reflection.

Recognizing your own efforts **reinforces their value, even without external validation.**

---

3. Trust the Ripple Effect

You may never see the full impact of your efforts, but that doesn't mean they don't matter. Just because you can't see the ripples doesn't mean they're not there. **Your work, your kindness, your persistence—they all leave traces.**

Real Impact Happens in the Quiet Moments

Some of the most powerful things in life happen quietly, without fanfare.

- **The seed you plant today may bloom years later, unseen by you.**

- **The kindness you show someone may ripple through their life and into others.**

Not every effort will be noticed, and not every act will be remembered. But **that doesn't make them any less meaningful.**

Closing Reflection: Your Work Matters—Even When No One Sees It

The world may not always notice your hard work. **But that doesn't make it any less valuable.**

You are not defined by how others react—or whether they react at all. Your efforts matter because **you choose to do them,** because **you care enough to show up,** even when it's hard, even when no one is watching.

So, the next time you feel invisible, the next time your work seems to disappear without a trace, remind yourself: **The ripple effect is real.** Your efforts—seen or unseen—are making a difference. And that is more than enough.

Neuroscience Insight:
Our brains are wired for **immediate rewards**, which makes invisible efforts feel unsatisfying. The **reward prediction error** system expects recognition after hard work. When it doesn't arrive, it triggers disappointment, draining motivation.

- **Practical Takeaway:** Self-recognition and journaling small wins **trick the brain** into releasing dopamine, providing internal satisfaction.

Case Study: Mr. Thompson's Late-Night Grading

Mr. Thompson was the kind of teacher who never sought the spotlight. He didn't stand out at staff meetings or win teacher-of-the-year awards. His students rarely remembered his name at reunions, and his classroom walls were bare compared to the vibrant posters and decorations of other teachers. What made Mr. Thompson special wasn't showy or obvious.

Every evening, long after the hallways emptied, he stayed behind in the dim light of his classroom. He carried stacks of papers home, carefully grading each one with more attention than anyone expected. He'd leave encouraging notes in the margins: "Great effort—keep going!" or "I see real potential here." He believed that his students' growth mattered, even if it wasn't reflected in test scores.

Mr. Thompson knew that most of these students wouldn't notice his effort right away. They wouldn't see how carefully he chose his words to inspire instead of discourage. They wouldn't know how much he worried about those who struggled. But he kept showing up, night after night, quietly believing that even small encouragements could plant seeds for future growth.

The Invisible Impact

Years passed. Mr. Thompson saw class after class graduate and move on, never knowing if his quiet efforts had made any real difference. He often wondered: Does any of this really matter? He loved teaching, but there were days when the work felt thankless. It's hard to stay motivated when your effort goes unnoticed, and harder still when you aren't sure if it's doing any good.

The Reunion

One rainy autumn evening, long after he'd retired, Mr. Thompson received an unexpected invitation: a reunion for a class he had taught fifteen years ago. At first, he hesitated. What would he even say to students who probably wouldn't remember him? But something tugged at him—maybe curiosity, maybe nostalgia—so he decided to go.

As he walked into the venue, no one recognized him at first. He stood near the back, nursing a glass of water, quietly watching former students greet each other with hugs and laughter.

Just as he began to regret coming, a young woman approached him.

"Mr. Thompson?" she asked, her voice filled with disbelief. "Is that really you?"

He smiled, nodding.

"I've been waiting years to tell you this," the woman said, tears welling in her eyes. "You changed my life."

The Ripple Effect of Encouragement

Her name was Elena, and she had been one of his quietest students. Mr. Thompson barely remembered her—she had always sat in the back of the class, kept her head down, and never raised her hand. But Elena remembered him.

"There was a time in high school when I felt like giving up," she said. "I thought I wasn't good enough, that I didn't belong. But you wrote something in the margin of one of my essays: 'You have a gift for writing. Don't stop.'"

Elena swallowed hard, trying to compose herself. "Those words stuck with me. They were the reason I didn't drop out. I carried them with me, even when life got hard. I became a journalist because of you."

Mr. Thompson's heart swelled. He had no idea. One sentence, scribbled in the margin of a student's paper late at night, had planted a seed that changed the course of someone's life.

The Lesson

Mr. Thompson's story is a reminder that invisible efforts often have profound, unseen impacts. Not every effort will be noticed. Not every encouraging word will lead to a visible transformation. But that doesn't mean it doesn't matter.

Many of the most important contributions we make—the kindness, the encouragement, the quiet support—go unnoticed. But that doesn't make them any less meaningful. Progress isn't always visible, and the ripple effects of small acts can take years to surface.

Mr. Thompson realized that the weight of invisible efforts isn't a burden—it's a gift. It's the quiet, persistent belief that showing up matters, even when no one is watching.

Chapter 5: The Power of Showing Up

Why Showing Up Feels So Hard

We've all had those days—the ones where the weight of everything feels too much. Maybe it's the fear that what you do won't make a difference. Or maybe it's the creeping doubt that **you won't be good enough.** Whatever the reason, it's easier to stay on the sidelines. Why try if you're not guaranteed success?

But here's the truth: **Success isn't built in leaps—it's built in small, imperfect steps.** And it begins with one of the hardest, simplest actions of all: **just showing up.**

How Resistance Holds You Back

There's a reason showing up feels like an uphill climb—your brain is wired to **avoid discomfort.** Whether it's the discomfort of failure, fear of judgment, or just the overwhelm of starting something new, **resistance kicks in.**

We tell ourselves: *I'll start tomorrow. I'll go to the gym when I feel more motivated. I'll write when I have a better idea.* But waiting for the "right moment" is a trap—because **motivation follows action, not the other way**

around. The only way to unlock momentum is to **take the first step.**

The Courage of Small Beginnings

We tend to underestimate the value of **small starts.** We assume that if we're not going all-in, it's not worth doing at all. But **showing up, even imperfectly, has a power that compounds over time.**

- **A single workout** isn't going to make you fit—but showing up at the gym, even for 10 minutes, creates a habit.

- **Writing a single paragraph** won't finish the novel—but showing up at the page makes you a writer.

- **A short conversation** won't solve everything—but showing up to listen strengthens relationships.

It's **not about doing it perfectly**—it's about being there, again and again, until small moments add up to something meaningful.

Consistency Over Perfection

One of the most powerful shifts you can make is to focus on **consistency rather than perfection.** Too often, we wait until we feel ready—until we think we can do something perfectly. But perfection is an illusion.

Progress only happens when we show up, flaws and all.

Think about people you admire—creators, athletes, entrepreneurs. What sets them apart isn't that they never failed. **It's that they kept showing up** through failure, doubt, and difficulty.

The truth is, **progress isn't linear.** Some days you'll take two steps forward and one step back. Some days, just getting out of bed will be your win. And that's okay—**showing up, no matter how small the effort, is still progress.**

The Science of Showing Up: How Small Actions Build Momentum

From a **neuroscience perspective**, every time you show up—no matter how imperfectly—you **reinforce neural pathways** that make the action easier over time. **Repetition rewires the brain,** strengthening habits and making it easier to show up again the next time.

This is called **the compounding effect:**

- **Each small action builds on the last.**

- **Each repetition creates momentum.**

- **Each step, no matter how small, brings you closer to your goal.**

By focusing on **small wins**, you create a feedback loop: every time you show up, you get a little more momentum—and the more momentum you have, the easier it becomes to keep going.

Why Showing Up Matters—Even When No One Notices

You might think: *If no one sees my effort, does it really matter?*

The answer is: **Yes. It matters deeply.**

You are **not defined by who is watching or how many people applaud your work.** Your effort matters because **you showed up for yourself**—because you honored the commitment to try, even when no one else knew about it.

And here's the beautiful part: **Showing up creates ripples.**

- Every time you show up, you inspire someone else—whether they tell you or not.

- Every time you take a step, you build resilience.

- Every act of persistence, no matter how small, strengthens the foundation beneath you.

The Myth of the Big Moment

Society loves stories of **overnight success.** We're told that big moments—awards, promotions, breakthroughs—are the moments that matter most. But

big moments are built on small ones. The world sees the result, but **you know the effort it took to get there.**

The truth is, **the magic isn't in the breakthrough—it's in the showing up that came before it.** The magic is in the mornings you pushed through doubt, the late nights you stayed focused, the small wins that no one else saw.

Action Step: Show Up for Five Minutes

If you're struggling to show up, start small. **Pick one thing you can do for just five minutes today.**

- Write a few lines in your journal.

- Move your body—stretch, walk, or dance.

- Reach out to someone you care about, even with a short text.

It doesn't matter what it is, as long as you **show up.** The goal isn't perfection—it's momentum. And once you start, you'll find that **the hardest part was just beginning.**

Closing Thought: The Power Is in the Showing Up

You don't need to be perfect. You don't need to have it all figured out. **You just need to show up.**

Every small effort you make is a seed. And while it might not bloom right away, **it's growing beneath the surface.** One day, you'll look back and realize that every small step—every moment you thought didn't matter—was part of something bigger.

So, what small step can you take today? **What would it look like to show up for yourself, right now, exactly as you are?**

Because in the end, **the power isn't in the outcome— it's in the act of showing up.**

Neuroscience Insight:
The **brain's basal ganglia** control habits and behavior repetition. Showing up consistently—even in small ways—strengthens these pathways, making actions feel easier over time. This process is called **habit-loop reinforcement.**

- **Practical Takeaway:** Repeating even tiny actions regularly builds habits that require **less cognitive effort** as time passes.

Case Study: Ben's Ten-Minute Jog

Ben didn't think of himself as the athletic type. In fact, the last time he'd intentionally exercised was years ago, back in high school gym class. But at thirty-five, his body had begun to feel the effects of a sedentary lifestyle. His back hurt from sitting at a desk all day, and he often found himself out of breath after climbing just a flight of stairs.

One morning, after stepping on the scale and seeing a number higher than he had ever imagined, something inside Ben snapped. He knew he needed to change, but the idea of overhauling his lifestyle felt overwhelming. Going to the gym sounded terrifying, and the fitness programs he saw online promised complicated routines that seemed designed for someone much more fit than he was. Where would he even begin?

Ben sat at the kitchen table, staring at his sneakers. He didn't want to fail—again. But what if, he thought, he could do just one small thing today?

The First Step

Ben put on his sneakers and set a simple goal: Just jog for ten minutes. No plans to become a marathon runner, no fancy fitness trackers—just ten minutes around the block.

The first few minutes were rough. His legs ached, his breath came in ragged gasps, and he felt painfully self-conscious as he jogged past other runners who seemed to glide effortlessly. His mind whispered: You're too out of shape for this. What's the point?

But he didn't stop. He told himself, Just ten minutes. You can stop after that. And when he finally reached his front door, panting and sweating, something surprising happened. For the first time in a long time, he felt proud of himself.

It wasn't much, but he had shown up.

Momentum Through Consistency

The next day, Ben laced up his sneakers again. The jog felt just as difficult, and the voice in his head still nagged at him: What's the point of running for just ten minutes? But Ben ignored it and kept going.

Over the next few weeks, those ten-minute jogs became part of his routine. Some days were harder than others— there were mornings when he barely dragged himself out the door, and rainy days when he questioned why he even bothered. But each time he showed up, it felt a little easier.

And before long, ten minutes turned into twenty. Twenty turned into thirty. Ben's breathing improved, and his legs grew stronger. What once felt like an impossible task had become a part of his day—just like brushing his teeth or making coffee.

The Unexpected Payoff

Ben wasn't just getting fitter—he was changing in ways he hadn't expected. The simple act of showing up every day built something more than stamina: it built trust in himself.

For years, Ben had struggled with self-doubt, setting big goals only to give up after the first few setbacks. But with each jog—no matter how short—he was proving to himself that he could follow through. That he could keep promises to himself, even when it was hard.

And that trust began to spill over into other areas of his life. He applied for a new job he'd been too afraid to pursue before. He reached out to old friends he hadn't spoken to in years. He started showing up for himself in ways that had nothing to do with running.

The Power of Showing Up

Ben's story isn't about becoming a world-class athlete or achieving perfect fitness. It's about discovering the power of small, consistent efforts.

Ben learned that progress doesn't come from grand gestures or sudden transformations. It comes from showing up, day after day, even when you don't feel like it. Some days will be harder than others, and the results won't always be visible right away. But over time, the act of showing up creates momentum—and momentum changes everything.

The Lesson

Ben's ten-minute jogs taught him a powerful lesson: You don't need to do everything perfectly. You just need to start. What matters isn't how far you go—it's that you keep moving forward, even in small ways.

Each time Ben tied his shoes and headed out the door, he built momentum. And that momentum carried him toward a better version of himself—not just physically, but emotionally too.

Ben realized that the hardest part wasn't running—it was showing up. But once you show up, everything else gets a little easier.

Chapter 6: The Hidden Courage of Everyday Life

What Courage Really Looks Like

When we think of courage, we often imagine grand acts—**heroic rescues, life-changing decisions, or public victories.** But the truth is, courage isn't always loud. Most of the time, it's **quiet, unremarkable, and unseen.**

It's the single mother waking up at 5 a.m. to get her kids ready for school, even though she's exhausted. It's the employee sitting down at their desk, choosing to try again after a tough week. It's the student raising their hand in class, despite the fear of looking foolish.

These moments may not feel like courage, but **they are.** Every time you choose to **show up in the face of discomfort or fear**, you're practicing courage—whether or not anyone notices.

Why Everyday Courage Matters

Courage isn't about the size of the action—it's about **doing what's hard in the moment.** And for many of us, the hardest battles aren't fought on grand stages—they're fought in the **quiet moments of ordinary life.**

- **Choosing kindness** when it's easier to be indifferent.

- **Staying committed** to your goals when progress feels slow.

- **Facing your fears** even when you don't feel ready.

Everyday courage matters because **it builds resilience.** Every time you push through doubt or fear, you strengthen the muscles you'll need to tackle bigger challenges down the road. **Small acts of bravery accumulate over time**, creating a foundation of strength that can carry you through life's most difficult moments.

How Fear Disguises Itself

Fear rarely announces itself loudly. Instead, it shows up as **self-doubt, procrastination, or perfectionism.** It whispers:

- *"What if I fail?"*

- *"What if I embarrass myself?"*

- *"What if I'm not good enough?"*

The tricky thing about fear is that it often disguises itself as **rational caution.** It convinces you to wait for the perfect moment, the right opportunity, or more certainty. But **perfect moments don't exist.** The only way to overcome fear is to **act in spite of it.**

The Courage to Start Again

One of the most underrated forms of courage is **the courage to begin again.** It's easy to show up when things are going well, when you feel motivated, or when success seems likely. **The real test comes when you stumble—when you fail, lose momentum, or feel like giving up.**

Starting again after a setback requires **humility and hope**—the belief that even though things didn't work out the first time, it's still worth trying. **This kind of courage isn't flashy, but it's powerful.** Every time you start again, you send a message to yourself: **I am not defined by my failures.**

Action Step: Find the Courage in Your Day

Take a moment to reflect: **What's one small, courageous act you can take today?** It doesn't need to be dramatic—just something that moves you forward, even if only a little.

- Maybe it's **having a difficult conversation** you've been avoiding.

- Maybe it's **trying again** on a project that feels overwhelming.

- Maybe it's simply **getting out of bed** on a tough day.

Whatever it is, **recognize it for what it is: courage.** Showing up—even when it's hard—is an act of bravery.

The Ripple Effect of Quiet Bravery

The thing about everyday courage is that it often creates **ripples you can't see.** The kind word you offer a stranger, the perseverance you show in your work, the patience you extend to yourself—**these small acts of courage have an impact** far beyond what you can imagine.

Sometimes, just showing up gives someone else the courage to do the same. **Courage is contagious.** And by living bravely, even in small ways, you make the world a little braver too.

Closing Thought: You Are Braver Than You Think

Courage isn't always bold or dramatic. Sometimes, it's just **taking the next step, even when you're scared.** It's getting through the hard days, showing up when it's easier to quit, and believing in yourself, even when no one else does.

So the next time you feel like your efforts don't matter, or like the challenges in front of you are too much, remind yourself: **Every small act of courage counts.** And every time you show up, you become a little braver, a little stronger, and a little more ready for whatever comes next.

You don't need to move mountains today. **You just need to take one step forward.** And that, in itself, is an act of courage.

Neuroscience Insight:
Courage isn't just a character trait—it's linked to **neuroplasticity**. Each time we act in the face of fear, **new neural pathways form**, reinforcing the belief that we can handle discomfort. The **brain's anterior cingulate cortex** plays a key role in this process by managing emotional regulation.

- **Practical Takeaway:** The more we confront small fears, the more our brain learns to **handle stress more effectively**.

Case Study: Emma's Phone Call

Emma sat on the edge of her bed, her phone clutched in her hand. Her heart raced, and her mind swirled with doubt. What if they think I'm a burden? What if I sound pathetic? She had thought about making this call for weeks but always found a reason not to. Tonight, though, the weight of her silence felt unbearable.

Emma hadn't always felt like this. A year ago, she was the life of every gathering—the friend people could count on to cheer them up. But somewhere along the way, life had knocked her down. First came the breakup with her long-term partner, followed by a job layoff that left her feeling unmoored. Everything she thought she could count on slipped out of reach, and soon, she found herself withdrawing from friends.

Each day, she promised herself she'd reach out to someone—just one person—but fear kept holding her back. She told herself it wasn't the right time, that she'd call tomorrow. The longer she waited, the harder it became. What if they had moved on without her? What if they didn't care anymore?

The Breaking Point

That night, after yet another day spent in silence, Emma felt something shift. She sat cross-legged on her bed, staring at the blank walls of her apartment, and realized how lonely she had become. The isolation wasn't just around her—it was within her. She felt hollowed out, as if she had shrunk into a smaller version of herself.

Tears welled up, and her breathing became shaky. The ache inside her chest pressed harder, whispering that she didn't matter. But beneath that heaviness, a small voice urged her forward: Just call. It's okay if you don't know what to say. Just call.

The Call That Changed Everything

Emma scrolled through her contacts, her thumb hovering over the name "Kara." They had been close friends once—before Emma began to pull away. They hadn't spoken in months, and the fear of rejection gnawed at her. But before she could talk herself out of it, Emma tapped the call button.

The phone rang. Once. Twice. Three times. Emma's breath caught in her throat, and just as she was about to hang up—Kara answered.

"Emma?" Kara's voice was soft, concerned. "Is everything okay?"

In that moment, the dam broke. Emma couldn't hold back the tears any longer. Her voice cracked as she whispered, "I just... I needed to talk."

Kara didn't rush her or demand explanations. She listened. And for the first time in months, Emma felt the weight in her chest begin to lift. Just knowing that someone was there—that she didn't have to carry her pain alone—was enough.

The Courage to Reach Out

That phone call didn't solve all of Emma's problems. Her struggles didn't magically disappear. But it was a turning point—a small, courageous act that opened the door to healing. The hardest part hadn't been the call itself—it had been choosing to reach out in the first place.

Emma realized that asking for help wasn't a sign of weakness—it was an act of strength. It took more courage to admit she wasn't okay than it ever had to pretend that she was.

In the weeks that followed, Emma began reaching out more often—small messages, coffee invitations, brief conversations. Each interaction reminded her that she wasn't as alone as she had believed. And little by little, she began to rebuild her sense of connection.

The Lesson

Emma's story is a reminder that courage isn't always loud or dramatic. Sometimes, it looks like picking up the phone and admitting, "I need help." It's easy to assume that bravery only belongs to those who make bold moves or take risks. But the truth is, the quiet acts of courage—like reaching out when you feel most vulnerable—are just as important.

Emma learned that it's okay to not be okay. It's okay to lean on others, to let people see you in your moments of struggle. We aren't meant to carry our burdens alone. And sometimes, the bravest thing we can do is ask for someone to walk beside us.

Chapter 7: Decision Fatigue and the Fear of the Wrong Move

The Tyranny of Too Many Choices

You know that feeling when you stand in front of a menu, overwhelmed by options, and suddenly, something as simple as picking a sandwich feels impossible? That's **decision fatigue**—the quiet exhaustion that creeps in when your brain is overloaded by choices, big and small.

And it's not just menus. **Every day is full of decisions—** what to wear, what to eat, which emails to answer, how to respond to that text, whether to make the call you've been dreading. These choices might seem trivial on their own, but **together, they drain your mental energy**, making it harder to focus, act, or move forward.

By the end of the day, you're left feeling **exhausted from all the deciding—without having made meaningful progress on anything that matters.**

The Fear of the Wrong Move

But decision fatigue isn't just about being overwhelmed by choices. **It's also fueled by the fear of making the wrong move.**

What if you pick the wrong career path? What if you make a mistake at work? What if you say the wrong thing in a conversation? **Your brain interprets decisions as risks,** and even small choices can feel heavy when you're afraid of getting it wrong.

This fear creates **paralysis**—you get stuck in indecision, waiting for clarity or certainty that never arrives. And the longer you stay stuck, the harder it becomes to move at all.

Why Your Brain Struggles with Decisions

From a **neuroscience perspective**, your brain is wired to **avoid risk and conserve energy.** Each decision uses mental resources—specifically **glucose**—and the more decisions you make, the harder it becomes to make the next one.

At the same time, **your brain fears uncertainty.** It wants guarantees, security, and safety. This is why **small decisions can feel overwhelming**—your brain treats them as potential threats, magnifying their importance until even trivial choices feel monumental.

The Cost of Staying Stuck

The fear of making the wrong move keeps us in **limbo.** We convince ourselves that waiting will lead to better decisions—that with enough time, research, or advice, we'll find the perfect path forward. But **the truth is, waiting rarely helps.**

Every day spent in indecision **drains your energy, chips away at your confidence, and leaves you feeling more stuck.** Over time, it creates a loop of avoidance, where **doing nothing feels safer than doing something wrong.** But the cost of staying stuck is **stagnation.** And inaction, in the long run, often becomes the biggest mistake of all.

Breaking Free: Progress Over Perfection

The key to overcoming decision fatigue and the fear of wrong moves isn't to **find the perfect decision—it's to make imperfect decisions quickly** and learn along the way. **Progress doesn't come from always being right—it comes from moving forward, even when you're unsure.**

Here's how to get started:

1. Limit Your Options

More options don't lead to better decisions—they lead to exhaustion.

- **Set boundaries on your choices.** For example, limit your wardrobe to a few go-to outfits or create a morning routine that removes unnecessary decisions.

- Use a **"two-option rule"**: When overwhelmed, narrow your choices down to just two possibilities. This reduces the mental load and makes it easier to decide.

2. Use Time Limits to Avoid Overthinking

The more time you spend overanalyzing a decision, the harder it becomes to act. **Set a timer** for smaller decisions—give yourself 10 minutes to decide, then commit.

- For bigger decisions, try the **"72-hour rule."** If you've been stuck on a choice for more than three days, **pick a direction and move forward.**

3. Trust That Most Decisions Are Reversible

Most of the time, **decisions aren't as final as they seem.** If something doesn't work out, you can **adjust, pivot, or try again.** Knowing that most choices can be reversed takes the pressure off and allows you to act without fear of failure.

4. Make Micro-Decisions to Build Momentum

When you're overwhelmed, start small. **Make one tiny decision**—even something as simple as choosing what to eat or what to focus on for the next 15 minutes. **Every micro-decision builds momentum** and reinforces your ability to act.

The Freedom of Imperfect Action

The truth is, **you don't need to get every decision right.** The goal isn't perfection—it's **progress.** Every time you make a decision, no matter how small, you reclaim power over your life.

Think of your decisions as **stepping stones**—even the wrong ones move you forward by teaching you something new. In the end, **there are no perfect choices—only opportunities to learn and grow.**

Action Step: Make One Small Decision Today

Right now, think of one decision you've been avoiding—something small but manageable.

- Maybe it's **choosing the first task to tackle tomorrow.**

- Maybe it's **deciding how to spend your next 30 minutes.**

- Or maybe it's **reaching out to someone you've been meaning to connect with.**

Whatever it is, **commit to making that decision today.**
Remind yourself that **movement matters more than
perfection.**

Closing Thought: Clarity Comes from Action

You won't always know the right answer. And that's
okay. **Clarity comes from action, not from waiting.**

Every step you take—even the wrong ones—will bring
you closer to where you need to be. **The only real
mistake is staying stuck.**

So, make a decision. **Trust yourself.** And remember:
**The power isn't in knowing the right move—it's in
choosing to move at all.**

Neuroscience Insight:
Decision fatigue occurs when the prefrontal cortex
becomes exhausted after too many decisions. As
cognitive resources deplete, the brain defaults to safe
or easy choices, such as procrastination or avoidance.

- **Practical Takeaway:** Making decisions early in
  the day—when mental energy is highest—and
  automating trivial choices helps conserve
  cognitive bandwidth.

Case Study: Raj's Breakthrough

Raj sat at his desk, staring at two open job applications on his laptop. His current job was draining him—long hours, a toxic work environment, and a constant feeling that he wasn't growing. But every time he tried to make a move toward something new, he froze.

He had spent weeks researching companies, updating his résumé, and bookmarking job postings, only to feel more overwhelmed with each new option. What if I make the wrong choice? What if the new job is worse? The fear of choosing the wrong path left him paralyzed, stuck between too many possibilities.

Each day felt like a battle between action and fear. Raj would wake up with a sense of determination—Today's the day I'll make a move—but by the time evening rolled around, self-doubt had crept in, and he found himself exactly where he started: stuck.

The Weight of Decision Fatigue

Raj's indecision didn't just affect his career—it spilled into every part of his life. His mornings began with paralysis over trivial choices: Should he wear the blue shirt or the white one? Should he make coffee or buy it on the way to work? Each small choice chipped away at his energy until, by the afternoon, his brain felt like a tangled mess of options and scenarios.

He'd heard of "decision fatigue" before—the idea that the brain, like a muscle, tires after making too many choices. But knowing the concept didn't help him escape the exhausting loop. Each potential career move came with uncertainty, and uncertainty, Raj thought, was something to be avoided at all costs. He wanted a guarantee, something that would tell him: Yes, this is the right choice.

But life didn't come with guarantees. And the more Raj tried to figure out the perfect path, the more exhausted and stuck he became.

The Advice That Changed Everything

One Friday evening, Raj met his mentor, Daniel, for coffee. Daniel had been through several career transitions and was someone Raj admired for his calm approach to life. After venting about his frustration, Raj asked the question that had been haunting him: "How do I know which job is the right one?"

Daniel took a sip of his coffee and leaned in. "You don't," he said. "You're waiting for clarity, but clarity only comes after you take the first step."

Raj frowned. "But what if I make the wrong choice?"

Daniel smiled. "There are no wrong moves. Each choice will teach you something. And the worst thing you can do is nothing—because doing nothing is the only way you guarantee that nothing will change."

The First Small Action

Raj left that coffee meeting feeling unsettled but oddly hopeful. He realized he had been waiting for certainty that would never arrive. He was standing at the edge of the pool, staring into the water, but the only way to learn how deep it was... was to jump.

That weekend, Raj opened his laptop, took a deep breath, and submitted one application. It wasn't his dream job, and it wasn't the perfect fit—but it was a step forward. And the moment he clicked "Submit," something shifted inside him.

He felt lighter, freer. Not because the decision was perfect, but because he had taken action.

The Momentum That Followed

Submitting that first application broke the cycle of indecision. The next day, Raj sent another résumé, and a few days later, he had his first interview in over a year. With each small action, the fear that had once felt paralyzing began to lose its grip.

Raj learned that progress didn't require certainty—it only required movement. And with each step, the path became clearer. Some interviews went well, others didn't. He turned down a few offers that didn't align with what he wanted. But each experience taught him something new.

Within a few months, Raj received an offer from a company that felt right—not perfect, but aligned with his values and goals. And when he accepted the job, he knew that it wasn't the destination that mattered—it was the courage to move forward, even when he wasn't sure of the outcome.

The Lesson

Raj's story teaches us that waiting for the perfect choice is a trap. Life rarely provides certainty, and the fear of making the wrong move can leave us stuck in place. The truth is, clarity comes through action.

Raj discovered that there are no wrong moves—only steps that bring us closer to where we need to be, even if they don't lead exactly where we expected. The key is to start moving, even if the path ahead isn't perfectly clear. Because doing nothing? That's the only decision guaranteed to keep us stuck.

Chapter 8: Small Wins and the Power of Micro-Movements

Why Big Change Feels Overwhelming

When life feels stuck, **the idea of making a big change can feel paralyzing.** Start a business? Go back to school? Write a book? Even the thought of beginning feels impossible. And so, instead of trying, **you do nothing.**

The problem with big goals is that **they demand perfection from the start.** They loom so large that anything less than immediate progress feels like failure. So, we procrastinate. **We wait for motivation. We wait for the right time.** But big change doesn't happen in one giant leap—it happens in **small, quiet movements that build over time.**

The Science of Small Wins

Your brain loves **small wins.** Each time you accomplish something—no matter how small—it triggers a release of **dopamine, the brain's reward chemical.** This dopamine hit reinforces the behavior, making it more likely that you'll take another small step.

Neuroscientists call this the **compounding effect.** Each small action creates momentum, and that momentum fuels the next step. **The trick isn't to force** massive action—it's to create tiny wins that add up over time.

How Micro-Movements Work

Micro-movements are **small, manageable actions** that move you toward your goal. They're so small, **they feel almost invisible**—but they matter. Why? Because **they bypass your brain's resistance.** Your brain isn't threatened by a tiny action, so it's easier to start. And once you start, **you create momentum.**

The Power of 1% Progress

James Clear, author of *Atomic Habits*, talks about the **1% rule**—the idea that small, consistent improvements add up to something big over time. **If you improve by just 1% each day, you'll be 37 times better by the end of the year.**

The key is to **let go of perfection and focus on micro-progress.** It doesn't matter if the step is small—what matters is that you **keep moving.**

Examples of Micro-Movements

- **Writing:** Instead of committing to a whole chapter, **write for 10 minutes.**

- **Fitness:** Skip the hour-long workout—**stretch for five minutes.**

- **Decluttering:** Don't tackle the whole closet—**clean one drawer.**

- **Relationships:** Send a **quick text** to someone you care about.

Each micro-movement reinforces the habit of **showing up**—and before you know it, those small wins start adding up.

Why Micro-Movements Feel So Powerful

- **They're Achievable:** Micro-movements are small enough to start without resistance.

- **They Create Momentum:** Each tiny step makes the next one easier.

- **They Build Confidence:** Every win, no matter how small, **reminds you that you are capable.**

Action Step: Start with a 5-Minute Movement

Right now, **pick one small thing you can do in the next five minutes.**

- Organize one section of your inbox.

- Move your body for five minutes—walk, stretch, dance.

- Write down **one task** to focus on tomorrow.

The goal isn't perfection—it's progress. Once you take the first step, you'll find that the next step feels easier. **Momentum builds from movement.**

The Freedom of Low-Stakes Progress

One of the best things about micro-movements is that **they lower the stakes.** When the goal isn't perfection, **you free yourself from fear.** Every small step you take—no matter how messy or imperfect—**counts.**

Some days, the win will be tiny. Maybe you'll only check off one small task, or show up for five minutes of work. **But that's enough.** Every step forward, no matter how small, is progress.

Micro-Movements Create Big Shifts

The magic of micro-movements is that **they don't just create external progress—they transform you internally.** With each small win, you **build trust with yourself.** You prove, over and over, that you are capable of showing up—even when it's hard.

And those small wins? **They create momentum.** Over time, that momentum **shifts the way you think about**

yourself—from someone who is stuck to someone who moves forward, step by step.

Closing Thought: Celebrate Every Step

The journey to change doesn't happen all at once. It happens in **micro-movements, tiny wins, and small acts of showing up.** You don't need to take giant leaps—you just need to take **one small step at a time.**

So, what's your next small win? Whatever it is, **start now.** Because every step forward—no matter how small—is a step toward the life you want.

Neuroscience Insight:
Each small win triggers the **release of dopamine,** which motivates further action by creating a **positive feedback loop.** This mechanism strengthens **dopamine circuits** in the brain, making progress more enjoyable.

- **Practical Takeaway:** Tracking and celebrating small wins provides a **dopamine boost** that sustains motivation over the long term.

Case Study: Mary's Gratitude Journal

Mary's life felt like it had fallen apart. After fifteen years of marriage, her divorce came like a storm she hadn't seen coming. Her home, her routines, even her sense of identity—everything felt shattered. She spent most days in a fog, dragging herself from one chore to the next, unsure of what to do with herself. Friends told her that things would get better in time, but the future felt distant and impossible. How could she believe that joy would return when even getting through the day felt like a struggle?

One morning, her therapist suggested a simple exercise: Write down three things you're grateful for every day.

At first, Mary resisted. It sounded trivial—almost insulting. "I just lost my marriage, and you want me to write about what? Flowers? Coffee?" she muttered under her breath. But with nothing left to lose, she decided to give it a try. One week, she told herself. I can do anything for one week.

The First Few Entries

The first few days were awkward. Mary stared at the blank page of her journal, feeling foolish. What did she even have to be grateful for?

On the first day, she wrote:

My coffee didn't spill on the way to work.

The sky was clear today.

My cat, Milo, curled up next to me.

It felt small. Insignificant. But it was something. And for the first time in weeks, she had spent a moment focusing on what was right instead of everything that was wrong.

A Shift in Perspective

The next day, Mary sat down with her journal again. Finding three things didn't feel any easier, but she pushed through. She wrote about the little things:

A kind smile from the cashier at the grocery store.

A hot shower after a long day.

A text message from a friend checking in.

Each entry felt mundane—nothing worth writing home about. But something curious began to happen. As the days passed, Mary noticed her attention starting to shift. Instead of focusing solely on what was missing, she began to look for small moments to be grateful for throughout the day—as if her mind had become a radar tuned to notice positivity.

On particularly bad days, when the weight of sadness returned like an old friend, the journal became her anchor. Even on the worst days, she could find something—even if it was as small as the comfort of a warm blanket or the sound of rain tapping against the window. Those small moments mattered.

Building Momentum

After a few weeks, Mary noticed a subtle but powerful change: Her days didn't feel quite as heavy. She still had moments of sadness—grief, after all, wasn't a problem to be solved. But the habit of gratitude gave her a new lens to view her life through. It wasn't about denying her struggles or pretending everything was perfect. It was about making space for both joy and sorrow to coexist.

Soon, the gratitude practice became a habit she looked forward to. She found herself jotting down entries throughout the day instead of waiting until bedtime. Small wins became visible, and progress felt tangible.

One day, Mary wrote in her journal:

I smiled today without forcing it.

I laughed on the phone with an old friend.

I took a walk and didn't feel sad the entire time.

They were small victories, but they were victories nonetheless.

The Ripple Effect of Small Wins

Mary's gratitude journal didn't just help her survive the difficult days—it began to change the way she lived. She started noticing small wins everywhere. The effort she had once dismissed as pointless began to build momentum. Over time, those micro-movements became a source of strength.

She reconnected with hobbies she hadn't touched in years—like painting and gardening. She made time to meet friends for coffee without feeling guilty about not being "productive." And slowly but surely, her life began to feel like her own again.

What Mary learned was that small wins aren't small at all. They are the building blocks of progress, the quiet moments that accumulate into transformation. One entry at a time, she built a new version of herself.

The Lesson

Mary's story teaches us that progress doesn't always come in grand gestures. Sometimes, it's about finding joy in the smallest moments—the way the sun feels on your face, the sound of a loved one's voice, or a moment of peace in the chaos. Small wins create momentum, and momentum builds change.

Mary realized that life doesn't have to be perfect to be meaningful. Her gratitude practice didn't erase the pain of her divorce, but it gave her the strength to move forward, one small step at a time.

Chapter 9: The Emotional Aftermath of Change

Why Change Feels Both Exciting and Terrifying

There's a strange thing about change: **Even when it's what you wanted, it doesn't always feel good.** You imagine that once you quit the job, leave the relationship, or hit your goal, you'll feel nothing but relief. But instead, **you're left with this uneasy feeling—like something is missing.**

This is the part of change no one talks about: **Even good change brings loss.** When you let go of the familiar— whether it's a routine, a habit, or a place—you leave behind a part of yourself. And that loss, even if necessary, comes with grief.

Why Letting Go Hurts

Your brain craves **certainty and stability.** It finds comfort in the familiar, even if the familiar isn't serving you. This is why **letting go feels uncomfortable**—your brain is adjusting to the loss of what it knew, even if what it knew wasn't good for you.

The discomfort isn't a sign that the change was wrong. **It's a natural part of the process.** In fact, the unease that follows change is **a signal that you're growing.**

The Emotional Rollercoaster of Progress

Here's something many people don't realize: **Progress isn't a straight line.** After taking a step forward, you'll often feel like you've taken two steps back emotionally. This is called **the "emotional slump"**—a period where the excitement of change wears off, and you're left facing the messy, uncertain middle.

- **You leave a toxic job** and feel lonely without the familiar routine.

- **You move to a new city** and miss the comfort of the old one.

- **You break an old habit** but feel lost without the structure it provided.

These emotions don't mean you've made a mistake. **They mean you're in transition.**

Why Growth Feels Like Chaos at First

From a neuroscience perspective, **your brain is rewiring itself** whenever you create a new habit or change a pattern. But before new neural pathways fully form, you experience a **mental and emotional chaos—**

a tug-of-war between the old version of you and the new one you're becoming.

This in-between space can feel overwhelming. **The old ways don't fit anymore, but the new ways don't feel natural yet.** It's like standing on a bridge between two worlds, uncertain which direction to go. But here's the truth: **This chaos is a necessary part of transformation.**

How to Manage the Emotional Aftermath

The emotional aftermath of change can feel heavy, but there are ways to **move through it with grace and patience.**

1. Give Yourself Permission to Grieve

Even positive change brings loss. **Allow yourself to feel the sadness** of what you're leaving behind without guilt.

- Write about what you're letting go of.

- Reflect on the version of yourself that you're saying goodbye to.

Grief is a normal part of growth. **Honor it, but don't get stuck in it.**

---

2. Embrace the "Messy Middle"

The period after change often feels awkward and uncertain. **This is the messy middle**—the space between who you were and who you're becoming.

The key is to **embrace the discomfort** rather than resist it. Every time you show up in the messy middle, **you're building resilience** and reinforcing the new patterns you're creating.

---

3. Find Anchors Amidst the Chaos

When everything feels uncertain, **create small rituals or routines** that give you a sense of stability.

- Start your day with a walk or a journal entry.
- End the day with a cup of tea or quiet reflection.

These small anchors will **ground you in the present** and help you navigate the emotional waves.

---

4. Recognize the Value of Emotional Growth

Growth isn't just about achieving external success—it's about **emotional growth** too. Learning to sit with discomfort, managing fear, and embracing uncertainty are **skills that will serve you for life.**

The emotional weight you feel right now isn't a burden— it's **a sign that you're becoming more resilient, more aware, and more capable.**

Action Step: Create a "Letting Go" List

Take a moment to write down three things you are letting go of as part of this change—whether it's a habit, a belief, or a way of being. Next to each one, write a **positive lesson or insight** that came from it.

This exercise helps you **honor what you're leaving behind** while focusing on the growth it has given you.

Why Change Often Feels Lonely

One of the hardest parts of change is the feeling that **no one else understands what you're going through.** When you're in transition, it can feel like you're walking a path that only you can see.

But here's the truth: **Everyone feels this way at some point.** You're not alone in this journey—you're just in a phase that most people don't talk about.

Closing Thought: You're Not Done Yet—You're Becoming

It's easy to mistake the discomfort after change as a sign that you've made a wrong move. But the truth is, **you're not done yet—you're becoming.**

The unease you feel isn't a failure—it's the space where growth happens. Every emotional wave you ride, every awkward step you take, and every messy middle moment you survive is **part of your transformation.**

So if you feel unsettled, lost, or unsure right now, remember: **You're exactly where you need to be.**

Neuroscience Insight:
The **amygdala** interprets change as a threat, even when the change is positive, triggering emotional discomfort. Meanwhile, the **hippocampus**, which stores memories, creates nostalgia for old habits and routines, pulling us backward.

- **Practical Takeaway:** Normalizing the emotional discomfort that follows change allows us to **retrain the brain** to view uncertainty as growth rather than danger.

Case Study: James's Second-Guessing After Quitting His Job

James stood in front of the bathroom mirror, brushing his teeth slowly, lost in thought. Tomorrow would be the first time in eight years that he wouldn't walk through the glass doors of the corporate building where he'd worked. Eight years—gone in the blink of an eye. He had put in his resignation two weeks ago, determined to leave behind the long hours and soul-crushing deadlines. It was the right move—or at least, that's what he kept telling himself.

So why did he feel so anxious?

The Unexpected Weight of Change

When James had decided to quit his job, he had imagined feeling a sense of freedom, maybe even exhilaration. But instead, he felt an unsettling emptiness creeping in. On the day he handed in his resignation letter, his coworkers congratulated him with a mix of envy and admiration.

"Wow, man, that's so brave," one colleague said.

"I wish I had the guts to do that," another chimed in.

James had smiled, acting confident on the outside, but deep down, a small voice whispered: What if this was a mistake?

The Emotional Whiplash

The first few days after leaving the job were a blur. He slept in, met friends for lunch, and finally had time to relax. But as the days stretched into weeks, the novelty began to wear off. Without the structure of a 9-to-5 routine, James felt adrift. He spent hours scrolling through job boards, even though he knew he wasn't ready to jump back into another office job. What if I left too soon? he wondered. What if I should've stayed longer?

Each night, as he lay in bed, the second-guessing became louder. What if I don't find something better? What if I just threw away a stable career? Even though James had been unhappy in his old job for years, his mind clung to the familiar—because the discomfort of the unknown was even scarier.

The Emotional Rollercoaster of Change

Change—even positive change—stirs up a mix of emotions. The brain naturally craves predictability, and when routines are disrupted, the amygdala (the brain's fear center) kicks in, flooding the body with anxiety. James's emotional whiplash wasn't a sign that he had made the wrong choice—it was simply the brain's way of processing uncertainty.

But James didn't know that yet. All he knew was that he felt lost.

A Conversation That Changed His Perspective

One evening, James met his friend Alex for coffee. Alex had gone through a similar career transition a few years earlier, and James hoped for some reassurance. He laid out his fears: What if I can't find another job? What if I'm not cut out for something new?

Alex listened carefully before saying something that stuck with James: "It's okay to feel lost. Change isn't supposed to feel comfortable."

He went on: "When I left my old job, I felt exactly like you do—like I was floating without an anchor. But being lost isn't the end. It's part of the process of finding your way again."

The Power of Sitting with Discomfort

James thought about those words on his walk home: "It's okay to feel lost." He realized that he had been fighting his discomfort, trying to force himself to feel okay too soon. But change takes time. Just because he didn't have everything figured out yet didn't mean he had made the wrong decision.

So instead of rushing to fix everything, James decided to sit with the discomfort for a while. He allowed himself to feel anxious without judgment. He reminded himself that every meaningful change comes with a period of uncertainty. And slowly, the anxiety began to loosen its grip.

Small Wins Along the Way

In the weeks that followed, James began focusing on small wins. He took a freelance gig—not because it was a perfect fit, but because it kept him moving. He reconnected with old hobbies, signing up for a photography class he had always wanted to try.

And with each small step, the fear of change began to fade. The path ahead was still unclear, but James no longer needed all the answers at once. He learned to trust that clarity would come with time.

The Lesson

James's story shows us that the emotional aftermath of change can feel overwhelming, even when the change is necessary. Uncertainty is part of the process—and learning to sit with that discomfort is what allows us to grow.

James discovered that progress doesn't always come in a straight line. Sometimes, it feels like wandering through the dark, unsure of where you'll end up. But every small step counts, even when the way forward isn't clear.

In time, the path will reveal itself—but only if you keep moving.

Turn Your Small Wins into Momentum

You've already started to break free from the chains of indecision and fear, whether you realize it or not. Each small step you've taken has brought you closer to creating real, lasting momentum. And guess what? You're not stuck anymore—you're in motion.

Now, let's take that momentum and build something unshakeable. This is where everything changes, because momentum is the force that makes big results not only possible, but inevitable.

Chapter 10: Building a Life of Momentum

The Magic of Momentum: Why Movement Changes Everything

Momentum is one of the most **underrated forces** in life. **Once you're in motion, things become easier.** Tasks that once felt impossible begin to feel manageable, and progress seems to build effortlessly—one step leading naturally to the next.

But here's the thing about momentum: **It doesn't just happen.** You build it. One tiny action at a time.

The Myth of Perfect Progress

Many of us believe that the only way to make lasting change is to **get everything right from the start**. We think progress should be linear—a smooth path from where we are to where we want to be. But that's not how life works.

Momentum isn't about **being perfect**. It's about **showing up, stumbling, and trying again—over and over—until the small steps add up.** There will be setbacks, missed days, and moments where you feel like you're starting from scratch. But every time you move forward, even a little, **you strengthen the momentum you're building.**

Momentum Thrives on Consistency, Not Speed

It's easy to get discouraged when progress feels slow. But **slow progress is still progress.** One of the most important lessons in building a life of momentum is this: **It's not how fast you move—it's that you keep moving.**

Even the smallest actions, repeated consistently over time, can create massive change. Just like a snowball rolling down a hill, **the power of momentum grows with every tiny movement.** What matters most is that you show up, even when you feel tired, overwhelmed, or uncertain.

The Power of the Next Right Step

When you're building momentum, you don't need to know exactly where the journey will take you. **You just need to focus on the next right step.**

- **Feeling overwhelmed?** Break it down. What's the one thing you can do right now?

- **Afraid of making the wrong move?** Choose the smallest, safest step forward—just enough to keep the momentum alive.

The beauty of momentum is that **clarity comes from action.** The more you move, the more things will make sense. The path may not always be clear at first, but **you'll figure it out by moving through it.**

How to Build Momentum in Any Area of Life

Momentum isn't limited to career goals or fitness routines—it can be applied to **any area of life**. Whether you're trying to improve relationships, build new habits, or overcome fear, the principles are the same:

1. **Start Small:** Begin with one manageable action. **Big leaps are hard—small steps are sustainable.**

2. **Celebrate Every Win:** Recognize your progress, no matter how small. Momentum builds when you acknowledge your efforts.

3. **Keep Going, Even When It's Hard:** Momentum isn't about never stumbling—it's about getting back up when you do.

Momentum and Motivation: Which Comes First?

Here's something surprising: **Motivation doesn't create momentum—momentum creates motivation.**

Many people wait for motivation to strike before they take action, but the truth is, **motivation often shows up once you're already in motion.** It's the small victories—checking off a task, making it through a tough day—that spark the motivation to keep going.

This is why **the first step is always the hardest.** Once you're moving, the effort required to keep going is far less. **Action feeds motivation.**

Momentum Survives Setbacks—If You Let It

Setbacks are inevitable. **You'll miss days. You'll get stuck. You'll feel like giving up.** But here's the good news: **Momentum doesn't disappear the moment you stumble.**

Think of momentum like a spinning wheel. **Even when it slows down, it doesn't stop.** The key is to keep nudging it forward—one small movement at a time—until it picks up speed again. You don't lose momentum by falling down. **You only lose it if you stop trying to get back up.**

Action Step: Build Your Momentum List

Right now, think of **three small actions you can take today**—one for each area of life you want to build momentum in.

- **Relationships:** Send a quick message to someone you care about.

- **Health:** Move your body for 10 minutes—walk, stretch, or dance.

- **Work or Creativity:** Write down the next task for your project.

These actions don't need to be perfect—they just need to happen. **The goal isn't to finish—it's to move.**

The Freedom of Living in Momentum

When you build a life of momentum, you experience a **sense of freedom.** You stop waiting for the perfect moment to start. **You stop overanalyzing every step.** Instead, you move through life with the confidence that each small step matters, each action builds on the last, and **momentum will carry you forward—even when things feel hard.**

Closing Thought: Keep Moving Forward

Life isn't about moving perfectly—it's about **moving forward, one small step at a time.** Some days, that step will be tiny. Other days, it will be a leap. But **every step matters**—because every step creates momentum.

When you feel stuck, overwhelmed, or uncertain, remember: **Momentum begins the moment you move.** And once you're in motion, everything gets easier.

So, what's your next small step? Whatever it is, **take it.** And then take another. And before you know it, **you'll be living in momentum.**

Neuroscience Insight:

Momentum relies on the **principle of behavioral inertia**—once you're in motion, it's easier for the brain to maintain that movement. The **dopaminergic system** rewards forward action, building momentum.

- **Practical Takeaway:** Start with **micro-movements** to build momentum and **keep reinforcing progress** with small, achievable goals.

Case Study: Mia's One-Paragraph-a-Day Writing Habit

Mia had always dreamed of writing a novel. For as long as she could remember, stories had filled her imagination—adventures, complex characters, vivid worlds. But every time she tried to put those ideas onto paper, self-doubt paralyzed her.

She would sit at her desk, staring at a blank Word document, waiting for the perfect inspiration to strike. When it didn't, she'd close her laptop in frustration, convincing herself she'd try again tomorrow. Tomorrow became next week. Next week became next year. Soon, the dream of writing a book started to feel impossible.

Mia told herself that real writers produced pages every day, crafting flawless prose with ease. And since she couldn't match that ideal, she gave up—again and again. Each failed attempt chipped away at her confidence. Maybe I'm not a writer after all, she thought.

The Decision to Start Small

One night, after another fruitless attempt to write, Mia stumbled across a blog post from a fellow author. The writer described how he had struggled with the same feelings but managed to finish his novel by committing to writing just one paragraph a day.

Mia was skeptical. One paragraph? That seemed too small to matter. But something about the simplicity of the idea stuck with her. What if she tried it? Not to write a novel overnight, but just to get something down—one paragraph at a time.

The next day, she opened her laptop and typed out a single, clumsy paragraph. It wasn't good, but it was real. For the first time in months, she had written something.

Building Momentum, One Paragraph at a Time

Mia kept her goal small: just one paragraph each day. Some days, she struggled to find the right words and barely managed four awkward sentences. On other days, the words flowed, and she wrote pages without realizing it. But no matter what, she showed up at her desk every evening, committed to the act of writing.

At first, the progress felt invisible. One paragraph didn't seem like much, and the novel still felt like a distant dream. But as the days turned into weeks, Mia noticed something remarkable: her confidence was growing.

She no longer dreaded sitting down to write. The blank page became less intimidating. With each paragraph she completed, momentum began to build. It wasn't about perfection—it was about movement.

The Unexpected Power of Consistency

Three months into her one-paragraph-a-day habit, Mia opened her writing folder to see how far she had come. There it was—40,000 words. Almost halfway to a full novel. And she hadn't even realized it.

Tears welled up in her eyes. She had spent years telling herself she wasn't a real writer because she couldn't produce perfect pages on demand. But that was never the point. The real magic was in showing up every day, even when it felt small.

Mia realized that momentum isn't built by waiting for inspiration—it's built through consistent action. The more she wrote, the more natural it became. Momentum wasn't something she found—it was something she created.

A Completed Draft—and a New Perspective

Six months later, Mia typed the final sentence of her first draft. It wasn't polished, and it still needed a lot of work, but it was finished. She had done it—one paragraph at a time.

Mia learned that progress doesn't need to be fast or flashy. Small, consistent actions are enough to build momentum. The key is showing up—again and again—no matter how small the effort feels.

Her writing journey wasn't just about finishing a novel—it was about learning to trust the process and herself. The simple act of showing up had transformed her.

The Lesson

Mia's story teaches us that momentum isn't something that happens overnight. It's built through small, intentional actions, repeated over time. Whether it's writing a novel, pursuing a goal, or creating a new habit, progress comes from showing up—even in the smallest ways.

Mia discovered that there are no shortcuts to success. But if you keep moving—even one paragraph at a time—momentum will carry you forward.

Chapter 11: Embracing Imperfection—Progress, Not Perfection

The Pressure to Get It Right

We've all been there—**stuck at the starting line, waiting for everything to be perfect before we move forward.** You tell yourself, *I'll start when I feel ready. I'll act when the timing is right. I'll try again when I know I can do it perfectly.* But perfection is a trap—**the more you wait for it, the further away it feels.**

Perfection whispers that **your work isn't good enough, your effort isn't enough, and that you're not enough—yet.** So, you hesitate. You plan instead of act. You wait instead of move. **And the longer you wait, the harder it becomes to start.**

Why Perfectionism Keeps You Stuck

Perfectionism isn't about doing things well—it's about **fear.** The fear of failure. The fear of being judged. The fear that your best won't be good enough. And while perfectionism might feel like a way to protect yourself, it often has the opposite effect: **It keeps you paralyzed.**

When **everything needs to be perfect**, nothing feels safe enough to begin. The longer you hold yourself to impossible standards, the more exhausted, overwhelmed, and stuck you become. **Progress slips away while you chase a version of "perfect" that doesn't exist.**

Progress Isn't Perfect—It's Messy

Real progress is messy. **It's full of missteps, false starts, and moments of doubt.** Some days, you'll feel like you're moving backward. Other days, you'll barely move at all. But progress isn't about being perfect—it's about **showing up, again and again, even when it's messy.**

Think about a baby learning to walk. **They stumble. They fall.** They don't get it right the first time, or the tenth. But they keep going, and before long, **those wobbly steps turn into strides.**

Progress is **learning by doing,** not by waiting. The only way to build momentum is to **move forward, one imperfect step at a time.**

Why "Good Enough" Is More Powerful Than Perfect

When you let go of perfection and **aim for "good enough,"** everything changes. Suddenly, it feels safer to start. **You lower the stakes**—you don't need to do everything perfectly, just well enough to move forward.

And here's the magic: **Most of the time, good enough is more than enough.**

- The conversation you're afraid to have doesn't need to be perfect—it just needs to happen.

- The workout you're dreading doesn't need to be intense—it just needs to get your body moving.

- The project you've been avoiding doesn't need to be flawless—it just needs to get started.

Perfection Is the Enemy of Momentum

Momentum doesn't come from perfection—it comes from **movement.** Every time you take imperfect action, you build trust with yourself. You prove that **you don't need to wait for the perfect moment—you just need to start.** And once you're in motion, everything becomes easier.

The truth is, **done is better than perfect.** A finished project—no matter how messy—beats an unstarted perfect one every time.

How to Embrace Imperfection in Your Daily Life

1. Give Yourself Permission to Fail

Failure is not the opposite of progress—it's part of it. **Each misstep teaches you something new.** Instead of aiming to avoid failure, **embrace it as a sign that you're trying.**

2. Focus on Effort, Not Outcome

Instead of measuring your success by the results, **measure it by the effort you put in.** Did you show up? Did you try, even when it was hard? **That's progress.**

3. Set "Imperfect" Goals

Try setting goals that **allow room for mistakes.** For example:

- Instead of aiming for a perfect workout routine, aim to **move your body three times a week—no matter how.**

- Instead of trying to write the perfect chapter, **commit to writing for 15 minutes a day.**

These "imperfect" goals **build flexibility into your progress,** making it easier to stay consistent.

Action Step: Take One Imperfect Action Today

Right now, **think of something you've been putting off** because you want it to be perfect. Maybe it's a project you've been avoiding, a conversation you've been dreading, or a change you've been postponing.

Now, **find a way to take one small, imperfect action toward it.** It doesn't need to be big—it just needs to happen.

- **Send the messy email.**

- **Make the phone call, even if you fumble.**

- **Write the first page, even if it's not great.**

The goal isn't to get it perfect—it's to get it done. **Progress begins the moment you move.**

The Beauty of Imperfect Lives

Life is not meant to be perfect—it's meant to be lived. **The beauty lies in the imperfection, in the moments where things don't go as planned but still turn out okay.**

You don't need to be flawless to make an impact. **You just need to be present.**

And here's the secret: **Imperfection is what makes life interesting.** The mess, the detours, the stumbles along the way—**they are part of the story.** They are what make your progress real, honest, and meaningful.

Closing Thought: Perfect Isn't the Goal—Progress Is

The next time perfection whispers that you're not good enough, that your work isn't ready, or that you need to wait just a little longer—**ignore it.**

Start where you are, with what you have. Take one imperfect step today, and then take another tomorrow.

Because life isn't about getting everything right. **It's about moving forward, one messy, imperfect, beautiful step at a time.**

Perfectionism activates the **anterior cingulate cortex**, which is involved in error detection. Overactivation of this region creates a loop of **self-criticism and anxiety**. The brain becomes hyper-focused on mistakes rather than progress.

- **Practical Takeaway:** Practicing **self-compassion** reduces the brain's error response, helping us focus on **progress instead of perfection**.

Case Study: David's Struggle with Perfectionism

David had always been his own harshest critic. Ever since he was a kid, he had felt a need to get everything exactly right—whether it was school projects, artwork, or even organizing his bookshelves. If something wasn't perfect, it wasn't worth doing. And over the years, that mindset followed him into adulthood, shaping his career and relationships.

Now in his late 30s, David's perfectionism was starting to wear him down. At work, he found himself constantly reworking projects, obsessing over the smallest details that no one else noticed. His coworkers admired his precision, but his deadlines often slipped because he refused to submit anything that didn't meet his impossibly high standards. Even simple tasks, like drafting an email, became draining rituals of rewriting and second-guessing every word.

David loved to draw—art had once been his way of unwinding—but now, he rarely picked up a pencil. Every time he tried to start a sketch, he'd freeze, convinced that his work would never be good enough. Eventually, he stopped trying altogether, leaving his sketchbook untouched for months.

The Breaking Point

One Sunday morning, David sat at his kitchen table, staring at the stack of art supplies he hadn't touched in ages. He wanted to draw, but the fear of failing stopped him. What if the drawing turned out poorly? What if it didn't match the vision in his head?

Frustrated with himself, David slammed the sketchbook shut and muttered: Why bother if it's going to suck? The weight of his own expectations was crushing his creativity.

Later that day, he met his sister, Jess, for coffee. Jess was an artist too, though her approach to creativity was the opposite of David's—she embraced imperfection. Her paintings were messy, colorful, and spontaneous. And people loved them.

David envied her ability to create without fear. During their conversation, Jess noticed his frustration and asked, "When did art stop being fun for you?"

Her question caught David off guard. When had art become another chore, another task to be done perfectly?

Letting Go of Perfection

That night, David sat down at his desk, determined to do something different. He picked up a pencil and promised himself one thing: I don't care how this drawing turns out. I just want to enjoy it.

At first, it felt uncomfortable—the critic in his mind whispered that the lines weren't straight enough, the proportions were off. But David kept going, deliberately scribbling and making messy strokes. He didn't erase a single mistake.

By the end of the night, he had filled an entire page with sketches. They weren't perfect, but for the first time in a long time, David didn't care. The act of drawing for the joy of it—without pressure or expectations—felt like a weight lifting off his shoulders.

The Shift Toward Progress

Over the next few weeks, David made a habit of creating without judgment. Some days, he spent hours sketching; other days, he only managed a few rough lines. But he kept showing up, enjoying the process instead of obsessing over the outcome.

He even started applying the same mindset to other areas of his life. At work, he stopped chasing perfection and learned to let go once a project was good enough. He found that submitting work on time—imperfect though it may be—was better than endlessly striving for perfection. His productivity improved, and his stress levels dropped.

The Lesson: Progress Over Perfection

David's story is a reminder that perfection isn't the goal—progress is. The fear of making mistakes often stifles creativity and prevents us from moving forward. But when we embrace imperfection, we free ourselves to explore, experiment, and grow.

David learned that the real magic lies in the process, not the outcome. The messy sketches, the rough drafts, the flawed attempts—these are all part of the journey. Progress isn't about getting everything right—it's about moving forward, one imperfect step at a time.

Chapter 12: Designing a Life That Feels Right—Not Just Looks Right

The Trap of Living for Appearances

In today's world, it's easy to get caught up in **building a life that looks impressive from the outside.** Social media makes it tempting to focus on how your life looks to others: the perfect vacation photos, the promotion announcement, the curated success. **We create highlight reels**, hoping that if we look successful enough, we'll feel happy.

But appearances can only take you so far. **There's a difference between a life that looks good and a life that feels right.** And if you've ever reached a goal or milestone, only to feel empty afterward, you know what I mean.

It's possible to **check off every box**—career, relationship, material success—and still feel like something's missing. **External success isn't the same as fulfillment.**

What Happens When Your Outer Life Doesn't Match Your Inner Life

Living a life that **feels right requires alignment—** between what you value, how you spend your time, and the choices you make every day. But when your life revolves around appearances or external achievements, **misalignment creeps in.** You might look successful on the surface, but deep down, **you feel disconnected from yourself.**

This kind of disconnection creates:

- **Burnout:** From pursuing things that don't truly matter to you.

- **Anxiety:** From constantly comparing your life to others.

- **Restlessness:** From feeling like you're always chasing the next thing, but never arriving.

The truth is, **you can't build a meaningful life by following someone else's map.** Your life needs to reflect **who you are**, not who the world expects you to be.

How to Identify What Feels Right for You

Designing a life that feels right means getting **clear about your values.** The question isn't "What should I want?" but **"What do I truly care about?"**

1. Get Curious About What Brings You Joy

- When do you feel most alive?

- What kinds of activities make time disappear for you?

- Who are the people or experiences that leave you feeling energized, not drained?

Pay attention to the small moments—**they are often the biggest clues** about what matters most to you.

---

2. Redefine Success on Your Terms

Ask yourself:

- What would success look like if no one else was watching?

- What kind of life would make you feel fulfilled, even if it didn't impress anyone?

Success isn't about **checking boxes—it's about alignment.** A successful life is one that **feels right to you**, even if it looks different from what others expect.

---

3. Let Go of the "Shoulds"

We all carry a mental list of **"shoulds"—things we think we should want, do, or achieve.** But building a life that feels right requires **letting go of those expectations** and making choices based on what feels true to you.

- **You don't have to climb the corporate ladder if that's not what you want.**

- You don't need a bigger house if simplicity makes you happy.

- You don't have to say yes to every opportunity if peace matters more than productivity.

The Courage to Live Authentically

It takes courage to build a life that feels right—because it might look different from what the world expects. **Not everyone will understand your choices.** Some people might question why you're not chasing more, doing more, or achieving more.

But here's the thing: **You are the one who has to live with your life—not them.** The opinions of others **won't matter** if the life you're living doesn't feel meaningful to you.

Living authentically means **choosing what feels aligned with your values**, even when it's uncomfortable or inconvenient. **It means saying no to things that don't serve you, even when saying yes would be easier.**

Action Step: Create Your Personal Compass

Take a moment to reflect on the following:

1. **What are your top three values?**

2. **How can you incorporate those values into your daily life?**

3. **What's one thing you can let go of today**—
   something you're only doing because you think
   you "should"?

Use your answers as a **personal compass** to guide your decisions. When faced with a choice, ask yourself: **Does this align with my values? Will this move me closer to the life I want to build?**

Progress Is Living Aligned, Not Perfect

Designing a life that feels right **isn't about getting it perfect—it's about making small, intentional choices every day.** Some days, you'll get it right. Other days, you'll fall back into old patterns. But the goal isn't perfection—it's **alignment.**

Every small step toward alignment matters. The more you practice choosing what feels right, the easier it becomes to recognize when you're on the wrong path—and to course-correct when you need to.

Closing Thought: Your Life Is Yours to Design

No one else gets to decide what your life should look like. **You get to write the script.** The only question is: **What kind of life do you want to create?**

When you stop chasing what looks good and start building what feels right, **you unlock the freedom to live authentically.**

So, what feels right for you? What's one small step you can take today to move closer to the life you want?

Neuroscience Insight:
The **brain's reward system** (ventral striatum) is more engaged when goals align with **internal values** rather than external expectations. When we pursue what feels meaningful to us, the **prefrontal cortex and emotional centers** work in harmony, creating a sense of flow and fulfillment.

- **Practical Takeaway:** Aligning daily actions with personal values **boosts intrinsic motivation** and helps maintain long-term well-being.

Case Study: Anna's Story: From Corporate Climb to Simple Joys

For most of her adult life, Anna had believed in one clear formula for success: work hard, climb the ladder, and enjoy the rewards that come with it. And for a while, the formula seemed to work. By her mid-30s, Anna had checked all the boxes—an executive role, a corner office, a six-figure salary. On paper, her life looked perfect.

Her Instagram feed was filled with highlights—business trips to New York, rooftop dinners with clients, and sleek photos of her modern apartment. Friends admired her, colleagues envied her, and her parents proudly bragged about their accomplished daughter. But behind the polished exterior, Anna was exhausted.

Every morning, she fought the urge to stay in bed, dragging herself through long days filled with endless meetings, corporate politics, and an overwhelming sense that something important was missing. She had built a life that looked impressive from the outside, but it didn't feel right on the inside.

The Moment of Realization

The breaking point came one Sunday afternoon. Anna was sitting in a meeting with her team, planning for the next quarter. She glanced out the window, noticing a small bakery across the street, where a young couple sat sipping coffee, laughing together.

For a moment, she imagined herself in their place—no emails, no deadlines, just simple joy. The longing hit her like a wave. When was the last time I felt that kind of happiness? she wondered. The life she had built felt more like a prison than a reward.

That night, as she lay in bed, an unsettling thought crept into her mind: What if I'm climbing a ladder I don't even want to be on?

The Struggle of Letting Go

Walking away from the life she had worked so hard to build wasn't easy. For months, Anna wrestled with doubt. What would people think if she left her high-powered job to pursue something simpler? Would she regret giving up the status and security she had worked so hard for?

The hardest part wasn't the logistics of leaving—it was letting go of the identity she had built around her success. Anna wasn't just walking away from a job; she was walking away from a version of herself that no longer felt true.

Building a Life That Feels Right

Eventually, Anna made the leap. She quit her job, sold her expensive apartment, and downsized to a small house in a quiet neighborhood. With the savings she had built up, she opened a small bakery, something she had dreamed of doing for years but had always dismissed as impractical.

At first, the adjustment was difficult. She struggled with guilt, wondering if she had made a mistake. There were no more big paychecks, no fancy titles, and no colleagues to impress. But slowly, as she settled into her new life, something shifted.

Anna discovered that baking brought her joy in a way her corporate career never had. She loved the rhythm of kneading dough, the smell of fresh bread, and the smiles on customers' faces when they tasted her pastries. For the first time in years, her work felt meaningful.

The Real Reward

The biggest change, however, wasn't in her work—it was in how she felt about herself. Without the pressure to impress others, Anna began to focus on what truly mattered to her. She spent more time with family and friends. She found joy in small, quiet moments—morning walks, evening chats, and the satisfaction of creating something with her own hands.

She realized that success wasn't about what looked good on the outside. It was about building a life that felt right on the inside.

The Lesson

Anna's story reminds us that it's easy to get caught up in chasing a life that looks impressive to others. But true fulfillment comes from designing a life that aligns with your values and brings you joy—no matter how simple or unconventional it may seem.

Anna learned that letting go of external validation wasn't easy, but it was necessary. The life she built for herself wasn't glamorous, but it was hers—and that made all the difference.

Chapter 13: The Inner Critic and How to Silence It

The Voice That Holds You Back

We all have an inner voice—one that **questions, criticizes, and doubts** every step we take. It tells us we're not smart enough, not talented enough, not ready yet. It replays mistakes like a broken record and magnifies every flaw.

This voice is known as the **inner critic**, and if left unchecked, it can be **paralyzing. Perfectionism, procrastination, and self-doubt** often grow from this relentless inner dialogue. The inner critic convinces us that staying small and safe is the only option—and so, we stay stuck.

But here's the truth: **The inner critic is not you.** It's just a voice—one that has **developed over time** from fear, insecurity, and past experiences. And the good news? **You can learn to silence it.**

Where Does the Inner Critic Come From?

The inner critic doesn't appear out of nowhere—it is **a learned voice** shaped by early experiences, societal pressures, and fear-based thinking.

- **Early childhood criticism**: Growing up in environments with high expectations can lead to **internalizing harsh standards.**

- **Comparison and societal expectations**: Social media and cultural norms reinforce the idea that **you need to achieve more to be enough.**

- **Fear of failure**: The critic tries to protect you by **keeping you in your comfort zone**, even if it means sabotaging your growth.

The inner critic is rooted in **self-preservation**—it believes that **if it criticizes you first, you'll avoid the pain of external failure.** But the truth is, **listening to this voice blocks your potential.**

The Science of Negative Self-Talk: Cognitive Distortions

Cognitive Behavioral Therapy (CBT) explains that **negative self-talk stems from cognitive distortions**—patterns of thinking that are biased and irrational. Here are a few common cognitive distortions behind the inner critic:

- **All-or-Nothing Thinking:** Believing that if you're not perfect, you're a failure.

- **Overgeneralization:** Drawing sweeping conclusions from a single setback. ("I failed at this project, so I'll fail at everything.")

- **Mental Filtering:** Focusing only on your mistakes and ignoring your successes.

- **Personalization:** Believing that **everything negative reflects on your worth**, even when it has nothing to do with you.

These distorted thought patterns **fuel the inner critic,** making it feel impossible to move forward with confidence.

How to Reframe Your Inner Critic with CBT Tools

1. **Catch the Critic in Action**
    The first step is to **notice when the inner critic shows up**. Awareness is key—if you can identify the voice of the critic, you can **separate yourself from it**.

    -   **Ask yourself:** "Whose voice is this?" Often, you'll realize it's the voice of **fear, past judgment, or outdated beliefs**, not your authentic self.

2. **Challenge the Thought**
    CBT teaches us to **challenge automatic thoughts** by looking for evidence. Ask yourself:

    -   Is this thought **100% true**, or am I overgeneralizing?

    -   If my friend made this mistake, would I judge them as harshly as I judge myself?

    -   What's the worst thing that could happen— and could I handle it?

Challenging the critic's thoughts helps you see that **your fears are often exaggerated** and not rooted in reality.

3. **Replace the Thought with a Kinder One**
    Once you've challenged a negative thought, replace it with a **balanced, realistic statement**. This isn't about forced positivity but **shifting your perspective**.

    -   Instead of: "I'll never be good enough."

- o   Try: "I'm a work in progress, and every step matters."

This process—known as **cognitive restructuring—trains your brain to develop healthier thought patterns** over time.

The Role of Self-Compassion: A Powerful Antidote

Silencing the inner critic doesn't mean becoming arrogant or ignoring mistakes—it means **treating yourself with the same kindness you'd offer a friend.** This is the practice of **self-compassion**, a concept championed by Dr. Kristin Neff, a leading researcher in the field.

Self-compassion involves three components:

1. **Self-Kindness:** Speak to yourself with kindness instead of harshness.

2. **Common Humanity:** Remember that **everyone struggles**—your mistakes don't make you an outlier.

3. **Mindfulness:** Acknowledge negative thoughts without letting them define you.

When you cultivate self-compassion, **the voice of the inner critic loses its power.** You learn to **make space for imperfection** and progress, rather than getting stuck in judgment.

Practical Tools to Silence the Inner Critic

1. Create a "Critic to Coach" Journal

Use journaling to **turn critical thoughts into coaching opportunities**. Write down the critic's message and **respond as if you were a kind, encouraging coach.**

- Critic: "You'll never be good enough to finish this project."

- Coach: "It's okay if you don't have all the answers right now. Keep going—progress comes with time."

This exercise helps **shift your inner dialogue** from harshness to support.

---

2. Name Your Inner Critic

Give your inner critic a **funny or silly name**—something that makes it feel less intimidating.

- Example: "Oh, that's just 'Doubtful Debbie' showing up again."

By **naming the critic**, you **externalize it** and reduce its emotional grip on you.

---

3. Use Affirmations to Rewire Negative Thoughts

Affirmations aren't just fluffy self-help advice—they **rewire neural pathways** by reinforcing new beliefs. Create a list of affirmations to **counteract common critical thoughts**.

- "I am capable, even when I don't feel ready."

- "Progress, not perfection, is what matters."

---

4. Develop a Daily Compassion Ritual

At the end of each day, write down **three things you did well,** no matter how small. This trains your brain to **notice progress instead of fixating on mistakes.**

- Example: "I sent that email I've been procrastinating on."

- "I took a break when I needed one."

- "I showed up, even though it was hard."

The Long-Term Impact of Silencing the Inner Critic

Over time, **as you practice these tools,** the voice of the inner critic will become quieter. It won't disappear entirely— that's not the goal. The goal is to **recognize it, challenge it, and move forward anyway.**

As you retrain your mind to focus on **effort instead of outcome,** and **progress instead of perfection**, you'll find that **you become your own biggest supporter**. And when that happens, **the possibilities are endless.**

Closing Thought: The Journey to Self-Acceptance

Silencing the inner critic is an ongoing journey—one that requires patience, practice, and self-compassion. But every time you catch a negative thought, challenge it, and replace it with a kinder one, **you reclaim your power.**

Remember: **You are not your thoughts.** You are the person who chooses which thoughts to believe—and that choice can change everything.

Case Study: Sarah's Inner Critic and the Leadership Role She Almost Didn't Pursue

Sarah had always been the dependable one—the person who worked behind the scenes, making sure everything ran smoothly. In every job she'd had, she excelled quietly, without ever stepping into the spotlight. Over the years, she watched colleagues get promoted to leadership positions, while she stayed in her comfort zone, convinced that she wasn't "cut out" for more.

It wasn't that she lacked ambition—the dream was always there, just out of reach. But the voice in her head—the inner critic—had a way of whispering all the reasons she wasn't ready. You're not experienced enough. You'll embarrass yourself. Who would follow your lead, anyway?

The opportunity came in the form of an email from her manager. A team lead position had opened up, and Sarah's name had been recommended. She was stunned.

Her manager's words were encouraging: "You'd be perfect for the role." But instead of feeling excited, Sarah felt paralyzed. That familiar voice—the one she knew so well—took over: What if they regret choosing you? What if you mess up? It's safer to stay where you are.

The Battle with the Inner Critic

For the next few days, Sarah couldn't shake the nagging voice of doubt. Even as her friends and coworkers encouraged her to apply, her mind raced with worst-case scenarios. What if she got the job and failed? What if she proved to everyone—including herself—that she didn't belong in leadership?

Sarah began to make excuses to herself. Maybe the timing wasn't right. Maybe she needed more experience. But deep down, she knew these were just fears disguised as logic.

Her inner critic had kept her stuck for years, convincing her that staying small was the safest option. But now, faced with an opportunity that felt both thrilling and terrifying, Sarah found herself at a crossroads.

A Turning Point

One evening, feeling overwhelmed, Sarah called her mentor, Jane, hoping for advice. She confessed her fears: "What if I'm not ready? What if I fail?"

Jane listened patiently before responding: "Sarah, that voice in your head isn't telling you the truth. It's telling you the same old story it always does, trying to keep you safe."

She continued: "Everyone has an inner critic. But you don't have to believe it. You just have to take the next step—even if it's scary."

The words hit Sarah harder than she expected. Her inner critic wasn't trying to ruin her life—it was just trying to protect her from discomfort. But the cost of staying comfortable was stagnation.

The Small Shift That Made a Big Difference

The next morning, Sarah made a decision. She still felt nervous—her inner critic hadn't disappeared overnight—but she was no longer willing to let fear make her choices. She sat down, opened her laptop, and submitted her application for the team lead role.

Her inner critic whispered: What if you regret this? But this time, Sarah answered it back: What if I don't?

The Outcome: Reclaiming Her Power

Two weeks later, Sarah got the job. Her first few weeks as a leader were challenging—there were moments of doubt, missteps, and days when she questioned her abilities. But each time the inner critic showed up, she chose to move forward anyway.

Sarah realized that progress wasn't about being fearless—it was about learning to act in spite of fear. And over time, her inner critic grew quieter, replaced by a growing sense of confidence and self-trust.

The Lesson

Sarah's story teaches us that the inner critic will always be there, whispering doubts and feeding fears. But you don't have to believe it. Progress isn't about silencing the inner critic completely—it's about learning to move forward, even when the voice of doubt lingers.

Sarah discovered that the key to reclaiming her power wasn't waiting until she felt ready—it was acting before she felt ready. Each step she took, no matter how small, weakened the grip of the inner critic and helped her build the life she wanted.

Silence the Critic, Prove It Wrong

You've spent too long listening to a voice that was never meant to define you. Your inner critic doesn't deserve the power you've given it. Today, you get to reclaim that power.

Every small victory you've earned, every bit of progress you've made—those are louder than any criticism you've ever faced. You've learned how to silence the critic.

Now, let's go prove it wrong

Chapter 14: The Journey Continues

It Was Never About Arriving—It Was Always About Becoming

If there's one thing this book has shown you, it's this: **there is no perfect destination waiting for you.** No final version of yourself, no moment where everything suddenly clicks into place. The truth is, **life is an ongoing process of becoming—** a journey made up of progress, setbacks, growth, and self-discovery.

Somewhere along the way, many of us bought into the idea that **we need to earn our worth**—by achieving more, doing more, or becoming someone better. But the real journey isn't about becoming someone else—it's about becoming **more fully yourself**, one small step at a time.

The person you are today is enough. And the life you build moving forward doesn't need to impress anyone. **It only needs to feel right for you.**

You Are the Author of Your Own Story

One of the hardest things to accept is that **no one is coming to tell you how to live your life.** There is no one correct path to follow, no universal roadmap that guarantees fulfillment. **The good news?** That means you get to decide what your life looks like.

This book wasn't about giving you a formula for success. Instead, it was an invitation: **to pause, reflect, and take ownership of your story.** You are the author of every chapter moving forward. And the best part? **You can always begin again.** No matter how far off course you feel, **you have the power to start fresh**—right now, right here.

What Progress Really Looks Like

The biggest lesson in all of this is that **progress is messy.** Some days, it will feel like you're making huge leaps forward. Other days, even the smallest step will feel impossible. But every effort—**even the smallest micro-movement**—matters.

Progress isn't about **speed or perfection.** It's about **showing up for yourself, again and again, in whatever way you can.** When you stop measuring yourself by how much you've accomplished, and start measuring by how consistently you show up, **everything changes.**

There will be setbacks. Life will surprise you with challenges you never saw coming. But now you know: **Setbacks aren't the end.** Every stumble, every failure is a part of the process, a part of becoming the person you're meant to be.

Trust the Process—Even When It Feels Uncertain

The road ahead will not always be clear. Some paths will be easy to follow, while others will leave you wondering if you made a wrong turn. **Uncertainty is part of the journey.**

But now, you've learned that **you don't need to have everything figured out to move forward.** You've built tools—

like reframing your inner critic, celebrating small wins, and finding courage in everyday moments. These tools will serve you well, **especially when the road gets rocky.**

Remember: **The next step will reveal itself only once you take it.** Clarity doesn't come from waiting—it comes from action.

What Will You Do with What You've Learned?

As you close this book, ask yourself: **What will you do with what you've learned?**

- **What kind of life do you want to build?**

- **What habits, routines, and choices align with the person you want to become?**

- **How can you continue to show up, even when it feels hard?**

There is no single right way to answer these questions. But the act of asking them—**and the willingness to try, even when you don't know the answer**—is what makes the journey meaningful. **This is your life to design.** And every small choice you make will bring you closer to the life you envision.

Your Next Step Is Enough

Don't worry about doing everything all at once. **You don't need to fix your entire life today.** All you need to do is take the next right step—whatever that looks like for you. **It doesn't have to be perfect. It just needs to move you forward.**

Maybe your next step is simple. Maybe it's reaching out to someone you care about, starting a project you've been avoiding, or giving yourself permission to rest. Whatever it is, **trust that it's enough.** One step at a time, you'll create the momentum you need. **And the journey will unfold from there.**

Action Step: Write Your Next Chapter

Here's an invitation: **Take a moment to write your next chapter.** Not in the literal sense—though journaling can help—but in the sense of **deciding what kind of person you want to be moving forward.**

- What are the values that will guide your decisions?

- How will you measure success on your terms?

- Who do you want to show up as—especially on the hard days?

Write these thoughts down. Keep them somewhere close. **Let them become your compass** as you navigate whatever comes next.

Closing Thought: This Is Your Journey

No one else can walk this path for you. But you are **more than capable of taking the steps that matter.** You are equipped with everything you need—the lessons, the courage, and the resilience to keep moving forward. **Even when the road is uncertain, you are enough.**

So take a breath. Take a step. And remember: **The journey itself is the reward.**

This is your life. **Live it fully. Live it on your terms.** And trust that every step—no matter how small—counts.

This isn't the end. It's the beginning of something extraordinary. The life you want isn't waiting for you someday—it's being built right now, with every choice you make.

No more waiting for permission, no more doubting yourself. You've taken the first steps, and now, the only way is forward. You've got the tools.

You've got the courage. Now go use them and build the life you've been waiting for. It's already yours.

Note from the Author

Your Journey Starts Now.

As you close this book, I want to take a moment to say something important: Thank you.

Thank you for trusting me with your time, your energy, and your journey. Writing this book was not just an exercise in sharing ideas,it was a commitment to you, the reader, to help you find a way forward, even when life feels impossible.

I hope, somewhere between the pages, you found a spark. A new way of thinking. A small shift that brought you one step closer to the life you truly want. Because that's the heart of this journey: not giant leaps, but the courage to keep moving, one small step at a time.

But remember, this is only the beginning. Growth doesn't end when the final page turns,it carries on with every small action you take after this moment. The real magic happens when you apply what you've learned, when you take those small wins and turn them into big changes, day by day.

And if you ever find yourself stuck again, and you might, because life is full of twists and turns, I hope you remember that getting unstuck is always possible. You don't need to have all the answers. You don't need to move perfectly. You just need to take the next small step.

Thank you again for letting me be a part of your story. I'm rooting for you, every step of the way.

With deep gratitude and belief in your potential,

Antonio Garrido Caballero

www.ingramcontent.com/pod-product-compliance
Lightning Source LLC
Chambersburg PA
CBHW031254060726
47590CB00003B/907